Illustrator
Ken Tunell

Editorial Manager
Ina Massler Levin, M.A.

Editor in Chief
Sharon Coan, M.S. Ed.

Cover Artist
Larry Bauer

Art Coordinator
Denice Adorno

Creative Director
Elayne Roberts

Imaging
Ralph Olmedo, Jr.

Product Manager
Phil Garcia

Researcher
Christine Johnson

Publishers
Rachelle Cracchiolo, M.S. Ed.
Mary Dupuy Smith, M.S. Ed.

Blessinger

D1450329

1910-1919

Author

Dona Herweck Rice

Teacher Created Materials, Inc.
6421 Industry Way
Westminster, CA 92683
www.teachercreated.com

ISBN-1-57690-023-1

©2000 Teacher Created Materials, Inc.

Made in U.S.A.

Table of Contents

Table of Contents *(cont.)*

Introduction

The 20th Century is a series which examines the political, economic, social, cultural, scientific, and technological advances of the 20th century and introduces students to individuals who made history in each decade.

1910–1919 chronicles American life just before and after World War I. Political upheaval throughout Europe and other areas of the world culminated in the Great War; though reluctant to take part in the fighting, the United States did finally enter the war during its last months, helping to turn the tide of the conflict and aiding in the eventual success of the Allies.

As often happens during wartime, technology developed rapidly with the need for more expeditious transportation, more powerful weaponry, and heightened communications. For the first time in the history of warfare, mass destruction became possible. Fighting became less personal while it grew in efficiency. Bombs, submarines, poison gases, and trench warfare made this possible.

Paradoxically, while the people of the world were embroiled in war, the world of entertainment began to take enormous strides. Hollywood established itself as the center of the motion picture industry, and such box office draws as Charlie Chaplain and Mary Pickford were among the most recognizable faces in the world. The decade, like most times, was filled with contradictions, from the lives of the very wealthy—such as those who traveled on luxury liners like the *Titanic*—to the millions of immigrants who lived in poverty. America dreamed of better times while, for the first time in its history, more of its people lived in cities than in the rural areas that were once the backbone of the country. Perhaps most ironically, the United States entered the Great War under the leadership of one of the century's most significant pacifists, President Woodrow Wilson.

While studying the second decade of the twentieth century, you will find a variety of aids in this unit to help make your studies complete, including the following:

- ❑ a time line—a chronology of significant events of the decade
- ❑ planning guides—summaries and suggested activities for introducing the key issues and events of the decade
- ❑ personality profiles—brief biographies of important individuals of the decade
- ❑ world views—chronology and details of world events of the decade
- ❑ language experience ideas—suggestions for writing and vocabulary building
- ❑ group activities—assignments to foster cooperative learning
- ❑ topics for further research—suggestions for extending the unit
- ❑ literature connections—summaries of related books and suggested activities for expanding upon them
- ❑ curriculum connections—activities in math, art, language arts, social studies, and music
- ❑ computer applications—suggestions for selecting and using software to supplement this unit
- ❑ bibliography—suggestions for additional resources on the decade

To keep this valuable resource intact so that it can be used year after year, you may wish to punch holes in the pages and store them in a three-ring binder.

Time Line

	1910	1911
Politics and Economics	The Union of South Africa becomes a dominion within the British Empire. There is a revolt in Albania. George V comes to the throne in England. Korea is annexed by Japan. The NAACP is founded by W. E. B. Du Bois. The Mexican Revolution begins.	Fire at the Triangle Shirtwaist Company, resulting in the death of 146 employees, adds fuel to the rising tumult concerning labor conditions and practices. Mexican Civil War ends. The Russian premier is assassinated. Germany's Kaiser declares it is time for Germany's "place in the sun." The Turkish-Italian War begins. There is revolution in China.
Social and Cultural	The architecture of Frank Lloyd Wright becomes popular. The "weekend" becomes a popular American concept. The first Father's Day is celebrated in Spokane, Washington. The Manhattan Bridge is completed in New York.	Irving Berlin writes "Alexander's Ragtime Band." The Gordon-Bennett International Aviation Cup is awarded for the first time. Renoir, Matisse, and Klee are among the most popular living artists. The career of Gilbert and Sullivan ends with the death of W. S. Gilbert.
Science and Technology	Halley's Comet is observed. Arthur Evans completes the excavation of Knossos. The first deep-sea research expedition is made. The telephone comes into widespread use. Marie Curie publishes *Treatise on Radiography*.	Air travel reaches a record height of 12,800 feet. Roald Amundsen reaches the South Pole. Marie Curie receives the Nobel Prize for Chemistry. Charles Kettering develops the first efficient electric self-starter for autos.

Time Line *(cont.)*

1912	1913	1914
Arizona and New Mexico become U.S. states.	The federal income tax is introduced in the U.S. with the Sixteenth Amendment.	World War I begins with the assassination of Archduke Ferdinand of Austria. Germany, Russia, Britain, France, Austria, Serbia, and Montenegro are among the first nations declaring war.
Montenegro declares war on Turkey. Bulgaria and Serbia mobilize their militaries.	The Seventeenth Amendment—providing for the election of U.S. senators by direct, popular vote—is ratified.	U.S. Marines are detained in Mexico by the Mexican government. Political turmoil escalates, but the conflict ends with the resignation of Mexican President Huerta.
Woodrow Wilson is elected the new U.S. president.	King George I of Greece is assassinated.	
The German-Italian-Austrian alliance is renewed.	The Balkan War erupts. The stage is set for the first world war.	
Lenin and Stalin join forces.	The U.S. Federal Reserve System and Federal Trade Commissions are established.	
Carl Jung publishes *The Theory of Psychoanalysis.*	Post-Impressionistic and Cubist paintings are displayed in New York for the first time.	James Joyce publishes *Dubliners*, and Edgar Rice Burroughs publishes *Tarzan of the Apes.*
The *Titanic* sinks.	Zippers come into widespread use.	Charlie Chaplin first appears in a movie as the Little Tramp, his signature character.
The first successful parachute jump is made.	Henry Ford experiments with assembly lines for the construction of automobiles.	The American Society of Composers, Authors, and Publishers (ASCAP) is founded.
Jim Thorpe dominates the Olympic Games, but his medals are taken away when it is learned that he played semi-professional baseball.	The Foxtrot is the latest dance craze.	The Panama Canal is opened.
Cellophane is created.	Coal dust is converted into oil.	Peat is first used to fertilize.
R. F. Scott travels to the South Pole.	Einstein begins work on his general theory of relativity.	Robert H. Goddard begins experiments in rocketry.
Protons and electrons are detected.	The basic precepts of jet propulsion are introduced.	The first successful heart surgery is performed on a dog.
Cosmic radiation is discovered.	Vitamin A is isolated.	

Time Line *(cont.)*

1915	1916	1917
The first submarine and Zeppelin attacks are made.	The Sinn Fein rebel in Dublin.	There is revolution in Russia. The tsar abdicates. Lenin and Trotsky gain in power.
Italy joins the Allies and declares war on Austria-Hungary.	Tanks are used on the Western Front.	Mata Hari is executed as a spy.
The *Lusitania* is sunk.	The Austrian premier is assassinated.	Wilson gains a second term as president; his campaign had emphasized that "he kept us out of war." Shortly thereafter, the U.S. declares war and begins fighting.
Changes continue in Mexico with the new government of President Venustiano Carranza.	Woodrow Wilson sends peace notes to the warring nations.	
The U.S. Coast Guard is established.		
D. W. Griffith's *Birth of a Nation* and Cecil B. DeMille's *Carmen* are produced.	Carl Sandburg publishes *Chicago Poems*, and James Joyce publishes *Portrait of the Artist as a Young Man*.	The actress Sarah Bernhardt begins her last American tour at the age of seventy-two.
Marcel Duchamp creates a stir with the first Dadaist paintings.	The National Park Service is created in the U.S.	Charlie Chaplin becomes the first film entertainer to make one million dollars a year.
Tetanus becomes an epidemic killer of soldiers fighting in the trenches.	The first birth control clinic is opened.	The first jazz recordings are made.
President Woodrow Wilson gets married while in office.	The first Rose Bowl football game is played.	Bobbed hair becomes the latest fashion trend.
The first motor taxis come into use.	Gas masks and steel helmets are used by the German military.	The first professional baseball game on a Sunday is played.
The first fighter airplane is constructed.	Daylight Saving Time (called "Summertime") is introduced in Britain.	Sigmund Freud publishes *Introduction to Psychoanalysis*.
Ford develops a farm tractor.	Blood to be used in transfusions is refrigerated for preservation.	A one-hundred inch reflecting telescope is constructed at Mount Wilson, California.
The first transcontinental phone call is made in the U.S. from New York to San Francisco.	Underwater ultrasonic detection is developed to locate submarines.	

Time Line *(cont.)*

	Politics and Economics	Social and Cultural	Science and Technology
1919	The 18th Amendment to the U.S. Constitution (Prohibition) is ratified. The Peace Conference begins in Versailles, France. President Wilson leads the first meeting of the League of Nations (the forerunner to the United Nations). Benito Mussolini founds the Fascist Party. Woodrow Wilson wins the Nobel Peace Prize.	The Bauhaus is founded in Germany by Walter Gropius, revolutionizing the teaching of the arts. Picasso, Munch, and Monet are among the celebrated painters of the time. An endowment of 20 million dollars is left by A. D. Juilliard to establish the Juilliard School of Music in New York. The "Black Sox" scandal shocks the world of baseball. The American Legion is organized. Sir Barton becomes the first horse to win horse racing's Triple Crown.	The first shortwave radio experiments are done. The nature of cyclones is discovered. The atom is shown not to be the "final building block of the universe." Experiments are performed on a film system with sound.
1918	Woodrow Wilson proposes his Fourteen Points for international peace. World War I ends with the signing of the Armistice between Germany and the Allies on November 11. Home Rule for Ireland is abandoned by the British government. The former tsar of Russia and his family are executed. Women in Britain get the vote.	The United States Post Office burns installments of *Ulysses* by James Joyce. The United Lutheran Church (U.S.) comes into being. The New York Philharmonic bans the performance of music by living German composers. Airmail service is established between Washington, D.C. and New York and New York and Chicago. Daylight Saving Time is established in the United States.	A worldwide epidemic of influenza begins. By 1920, 22 million people will die. Excavations begin in Babylonia. Max Planck wins the Nobel Prize in Physics for his quantum theory. The true dimensions of the Milky Way are discovered.

Using the Time Line

Use pages five through eight to create a visual display for your classroom. Follow the steps outlined below to assemble the time line as a bulletin board, and then choose from the suggested uses those that best suit your classroom needs.

Bulletin Board Assembly

Copy pages five through eight. Enlarge and/or color them, if desired. Tape the pages together to form a continuous time line and attach it to a prepared bulletin board background or a classroom wall. (To make a reusable bulletin board, glue each page of the time line to oaktag. After the glue has dried, laminate the pages. Write on the laminated pages with dry-erase markers.)

	1910	1911	1912	1913	1914	1915	1916	1917	1918	1919	
Politics and Economics											**Politics and Economics**
Social and Cultural											**Social and Cultural**
Science and Technology											**Science and Technology**

Suggested Uses

1. Use the time line to assess students' initial knowledge of the era. Construct a web to find out what they know about World War I or the League of Nations, for example. Find out what they would like to know. Plan your lessons accordingly.

2. Assign each group of students a specific year. As they research that year, let them add pictures, names, and events to the appropriate area of the time line.

3. Ask the students to discover what other events were happening around the world during the second decade of the twentieth century. Tell them to add that information to the bottom of the time line.

4. After adding new names, places, and events to the time line, use the information gathered as a study guide for assessment. Base your quizzes and exams on those people, places, and events which you have studied.

5. After time line has been on display for a few days, begin to quiz students about the people, places, and events named there. Call on one student at a time to stand so that he or she is facing away from the actual time line. Ask a question based on the information. Variation: Let the students compose the questions.

6. Use the time line as a springboard for a class discussion; for example, who was the most famous or influential person of the second decade? How have the inventions of that time affected their lives today? How was life in those years similar to their lives today?

7. Divide the students into three groups and assign each group a different area: politics/economics, society/culture, or science/technology. Have each group brainstorm important related people, places, and events that lived or occurred during the decade, and then create a group mural depicting these important happenings and people. Get permission to paint a hallway or tape several sheets of butcher paper together to make a giant canvas.

8. Assign groups of students to make specialized time lines—for example, a time line of the construction of the Panama Canal, of the eventual destruction of the *Titanic*, or of the creation of the new film mecca called Hollywood.

1910–1919 Overview

- World War I began as a local war between Austria-Hungary and Serbia. As a result of conflicts in the Balkan states, the rise of nationalism, and a series of international alliances, it rapidly became a general European struggle. Eventually it was a global war involving 32 nations. The 28 nations known as the Allies and Associated Powers included Great Britain, France, Russia, Italy, and, eventually, the United States. The Central Powers consisted of Germany, Austria-Hungary, Turkey, and Bulgaria. Acts of heroism and tragedy filled the newspapers daily, and people on the home fronts focused their energies on "helping the cause" in whatever ways they could.

- Heroes and villains came to the forefront throughout the war and in its aftermath. Frequently mentioned names included Lenin, Rasputin, Mussolini, Lloyd George, Kitchener, Von Hindenburg, Mata Hari, the Kaiser, Tsar Nicholas II, Trotsky, Stalin, the Red Baron, General John J. Pershing, Bernard Baruch, and Herbert Hoover.

- Tanks, submarines, zeppelins, poison gas, long-range bombers, and fighter planes were used for the first time.

- Power in Europe and Russia shifted dramatically both during the Great War and as a result of its effects. New leaders offered hope to the impoverished and battle-scarred masses.

- Labor disputes continued. A tragic fire at the Triangle Shirtwaist Company killed 146 employees. That and other tragedies built momentum for enhanced labor laws.

- The call for women's rights, especially the vote, grew as the economy at home depended more and more on the work of women while the men were away fighting the war. The end of the decade brought victory to the suffragists.

- President Woodrow Wilson's Fourteen Points plan for peace included the formation of a League of Nations.

- Mexico faced a revolution in an effort to oust its dictator, Porfirio Diaz.

- Inventor Thomas Edison developed talking pictures, which would soon revolutionize the entertainment industry. In Hollywood, California, a film mecca was begun by Cecil B. De Mille. A small group of actors began a new company, United Artists, in order to produce films.

- The Indianapolis Motor Speedway held its first 500-mile race. The first winner, Ray Harroun, drove at the speed of 75 miles per hour.

- In 1913 the Sixteenth Amendment to the U.S. Constitution made income taxes legal. Three months later, the Seventeenth Amendment was ratified. It provided for the election of United States senators by direct, popular vote. Prior to this, they had been elected by their state legislatures.

- The Selective Service began its draft of young men for military duty.

- China saw its last emperor and closed the 260-year reign of the Manchu dynasty.

- The new luxury liner *Titanic* struck an iceberg on its maiden voyage and sank. Nearly 1,600 people drowned, due largely to a shortage of lifeboats on board.

- New Mexico and Arizona joined the United States in 1912.

- Jim Thorpe, a Native American, amazed audiences at the 1912 Olympics. Many considered him the greatest athlete ever. However, he was later stripped of his medals for having played semi-professional baseball for a short period of time.

- The Panama Canal, once considered an impossible venture, was opened in 1914.

- Kindergartens became popular in the United States, and several states added them to their school programs.

- Daylight Saving Time began in an effort to save electricity to help the war effort.

Introducing 1910-1919

On this page you will find some interesting ways to introduce the decade of 1910–1919 to your students. Keep in mind that these are suggestions only—it is not necessary to use all of them. Your project selections should be based on student needs, interests, and objectives.

1. **Sing Along:** Learn about popular songs of the decade. Teach some to the class or create a demonstration of the songs and their origins. Look to Americana songbooks as your source.

2. **Fashions:** The "pouter pigeon" look, with slightly dropped waists, full blouses, and elaborate hats, was at the peak of fashion during this decade, as were bobbed hair, pointed-toe shoes, spats, leggings, and skirt lengths raised above the ankle. Men's fashions changed little from the previous decade, although jackets and pants slimmed slightly, and the look of military uniforms began to influence style. Have students find pictures of clothing from this era. An excellent source are the paperdoll books published by Dover Publishing of New York.

3. **Artwork:** Display artwork either of the time (such as Picasso, Monet, Duchamp, or Klee) or that which reflects life during the time. Assign students to create their own artwork that is reflective of the decade.

4. **Hats:** Most people wore hats in public during the early twentieth century. Allow students to become haberdashers, creating their own hats befitting the styles of the era.

5. **Electricity:** Create a class display showing the evolution of electrically run products with origins in this decade. This may be as simple as a then-and-now bulletin board.

6. **Read Aloud:** Read aloud from classic literature of the time, such as Hugh Lofting's *Doctor Doolittle* books, G. K. Chesterton's *Father Brown* books, Willa Cather's *O Pioneers!* or *My Antonia,* or the poetry of Robert Frost.

7. **Guest Speaker:** Contact local colleges, universities, museums, and historical societies for potential speakers who are experts on the era. Have students prepare questions about the time period to ask the speaker.

8. **Interview:** Allow students to dress as famous people from the decade and, having researched their lives, to answer questions from the class as the figures might have done in a contemporary interview.

9. **Inventions:** The second decade of the new century, like the first, was filled with exciting new inventions. Research some of those inventions and discuss how they changed the lives of people around the world. Pay particular attention to the inventions brought about through war and how they affected the outcome of the fighting.

10. **Melting Pot:** Many people still consider the United States to be a great melting pot of world cultures. The decade of 1910–1919 saw a great deal of immigration and, therefore, the introduction of new cultures, languages, and ways of life into the mainstream of society. Brainstorm some of those cultures and their contributions to American culture as a whole. Discuss immigration of the time and immigration today. Also, consider the growing concerns of the time over surplus population and the need to curb immigration.

11. **Living During War:** As a class, discuss how World War I affected the day-to-day lives of Americans, and then compare those effects to the ways the war affected the lives of Europeans. Consider how life and history in the United States might have been altered if the war had come to American soil.

Discussing 1910–1919

Create student interest with a lively discussion. Suggested topics and some methods for implementing them follow.

World War I: World War I dominated the 1910s. Discuss the events that led to the war and America's resistance to participation. Debate the pros and cons of American involvement. Also, discuss how the war may have been avoided or if it was inevitable.

World War III: Discuss the state of the world today and the possibilities for World War III. Also, discuss what it may have been like to live from 1910 through 1919 with the tensions and results of war.

Unions: Many labor unions came into significant power during the 1910s in an attempt to combat unhealthy, unsafe, and unfair conditions in factories and workplaces. As a result of their work and the changing times, many new labor laws came into being. Discuss the role of unions and how they have helped to shape the labor conditions of today.

Daylight Saving Time: Daylight Saving Time came about during wartime for economic purposes. Research and discuss how it began. Then debate its value today.

The Movies: Cinema developed in leaps and bounds during the 1910s, creating a variety of the world's first film stars. What effect has cinema had on life and culture over the years?

Selective Service: Also known as "the draft," the Selective Service Act came into being in 1917. Discuss the draft and whether or not it should exist.

***Titanic*:** Among the most famous vessels of all time, the *Titanic*'s life was a short one. Its first and only voyage was in 1912. Discuss the tragic events of this voyage, and then discuss the likelihood of such an experience today. Remind the students that boats still sink and tragedy is not completely avoidable. However, much about safety has been learned throughout the century, some of it as a direct result of the *Titanic* disaster. Discuss how safety procedures have changed since 1912, and also discuss what individuals can do daily to protect their personal safety.

Income Tax: With the Sixteenth Amendment to the Constitution, federal income tax became law. Discuss the pros and cons of such a law. Discuss the uses for the money garnered through income taxation.

Mother's Day and Father's Day: Mother's Day and Father's Day became legal holidays around this time. Many consider these holidays to be predecessors to the myriad days we celebrate today in honor of certain individuals such as grandparents, secretaries, bosses, and teachers. Discuss whether or not such days should be set aside to honor these individuals. Do any such days take the concept too far?

National Parks: The National Park Service was formed during this decade. Consider the worth of such a service. Should lands be set aside specifically for preservation, or should all land be open for development? Discuss any pros and cons of the issue.

The Great War

Fought on three continents, the war that lasted from 1914 through 1918 was known simply as the Great War. When a second such war began, its name was then changed to World War I. Below are listed some of the major events of the war that tore nations—and the world—apart.

1911   Germany is growing in power, and the French and British are alarmed. The Germans send a gunboat to Agadir, Morocco, which is under French protection, resulting in the Agadir Crisis in which France and Germany narrowly avoid a war. France and Great Britain feel certain that Germany is a threat to world peace. Austria-Hungary and Britain increase their respective navies.

Turkish rule over the Balkan states is showing breakdown. Revolt seems certain.

1912   The Balkan states revolt against Turkey.

1913   Having defeated the Turks, the Balkan states begin to fight among themselves. Other nations take sides in their conflicts.

1914   Archduke Francis Ferdinand, heir to the throne of Austria-Hungary, and his wife, Sophie, are assassinated on June 28 while visiting Sarajevo, Bosnia (part of the Austro-Hungarian Empire). The assassin, Gavrilo Princip, is a Serbian. Austria-Hungary blames the Serbians and declares war on them and on Russia, which is fighting in defense of Serbia. Germany joins forces with Austria-Hungary, as does Turkey. The three are the Central Powers. Germans march through Belgium and attempt to take Paris. Belgium joins forces with Serbia, as does Britain, which has a treaty with Belgium. Russia, Serbia, France, Belgium, and Britain become the Allies. Germany's Kaiser calls for victory by autumn. The Allies are confident the war will end by Christmas.

Trench warfare is used for the first time in Belgium and France. The Allies halt the Germans at the bloody Battle of the Marne, protecting Paris for the time being. The Russian General Samsonov shoots himself after failing to invade Germany and losing 120,000 men to Germany as prisoners.

On Christmas Day in Ypres, Belgium, soldiers from both sides gather together peacefully, talking and sharing cigarettes. By the end of the year, there are hundreds of thousands of casualties.

1915   Germany uses chlorine gas in Ypres, the first time poisonous gas has been used in war. The Germans wear face masks to protect themselves.

Russia attempts to keep Germany out of Poland. Bulgaria aids Germany and helps them to overtake Poland and capture Serbia. The Allies fight to protect the Dardanelles Channel, which is a crucial passageway for the Russians. It is blocked by Turkey. They make several attempts from the Gallipoli Peninsula, but they repeatedly fail and finally withdraw. The Anzacs (Australian and New Zealand Army Corps), who have just joined the war, are particularly noted for their bravery at Gallipoli.

A British nurse named Edith Cavell, head of the Brussels School of Nursing, is executed by the Germans for helping British soldiers to escape.

The Great War *(cont.)*

1915 *(cont.)*

The British liner *Lusitania*, the largest passenger ship in the world, is torpedoed by a German U-boat (submarine) off the Irish coast. The ship is unarmed and carries nearly 2,000 passengers and crew members. Many die, including nearly 130 Americans. The Germans have orders to stop all supplies from reaching Britain; every ship is suspect. The United States is outraged, and many believe that President Wilson will not be able to keep the United States out of the war, although Germany apologizes for its error.

Italy joins the Allies and declares war on Austria-Hungary.

1916

The Battle of Jutland, the only major naval battle of the war, is fought, and hundreds die. There is no victor.

France experiences massive casualties at Verdun, where Germans use flamethrowers and gas shells. Meanwhile, the Allies attack at the Somme, attempting to relieve the soldiers at Verdun. However, nearly two million die.

Lord Kitchener, the British secretary of war, is drowned when his ship hits a mine. Kitchener is famous for his recruiting poster. David Lloyd George replaces Kitchener.

In September, the Allies introduce their new weapon: the tank.

Russia attacks Austria, gaining 60 miles (100 kilometers) and 400,000 prisoners.

President Wilson is reelected under the slogan "He kept us out of the war."

1917

The Russian people, tired of the war, begin to revolt. They blame the tsar for their two million casualties and impoverished conditions at home. V. I. Lenin and the Bolsheviks overtake the government and sign an armistice with Germany. Russia is out of the war.

In April, after three years of attempting to stay out of the war and bring peace to the world, President Wilson and the United States Congress declare war on the Germans. Public opinion is almost completely won over due to an intercepted telegram from the German foreign minister to his ambassador in Mexico. In it, the Germans offer to aid Mexico in recovering its previous holdings, now a part of the United States (Texas, New Mexico, and Arizona). Millions of Americans enlist in the U.S. Army and travel "Over There" to the Western front.

The Italians experience total defeat at Caporetto, where the Germans and Austria-Hungary gain huge areas of land. The surviving Italian soldiers retreat, leaving their weapons behind on the battlefield.

China declares war on Germany and Austria.

Germany creates the Hindenburg Line, a 31-mile (50-kilometer) system of trenches with concrete dugouts, barbed wire, and access to railroads for supplies.

Passchendaele, France, becomes the scene of one of the bloodiest battles in the war. It is fought in constant rain and mud, and the shooting is relentless.

The Red Cross receives the Nobel Peace Prize for its volunteer work on the battlefields of the world.

14

The Great War *(cont.)*

1918 President Wilson outlines Fourteen Points for peace, including the formation of a League of Nations to protect independence for all nations.

In the spring, the Germans leave the Hindenburg Line to make two offensives. The first is at the Marne, where the Allies once again defend themselves with heavy casualties. At the same time, they battle the other offensive at the Lys River in Belgium. The German general Erich von Ludendorff asks the Kaiser to make peace. Ludendorff is dismissed from his duties.

Thousands of American troops arrive in France. A series of Allied counterattacks result in victories. An Allied war victory seems imminent.

The ace German pilot, the Red Baron, is killed. Allies pay tribute to him and his skill, although he was an enemy.

Hundreds of Germans surrender in the face of intense attacks by Allied planes and tanks.

Turkey is defeated by the British, led by General Edmund Allenby. Lt. Col. T. E. Lawrence has been highly effective in the war against the Turks.

Austria-Hungary becomes a republic and is out of the war.

An epidemic of influenza strikes around the world, causing millions of deaths.

Nicholas, the former tsar of Russia, and his family are executed by the Bolsheviks.

At 11 A.M. on the eleventh day of the eleventh month, an armistice is signed by the Allies and Germany. The four-year war is over. France and Belgium have been nearly destroyed.

The United States comes out of the war with its land intact and its economy strong. It is in a favorable position to become a major world leader. Many European nations are devastated and impoverished.

1919 Terms for peace are agreed upon by the victorious nations at the Palace of Versailles in Paris, France. President Wilson urges the creation of a League of Nations. The German chancellor resigns, refusing to sign the treaty. It calls for Germany to pay 33 million dollars to the Allies in reparations and to reduce its army and arsenal of weapons. On June 28, two German representatives silently enter the palace and sign the treaty; they leave without saying a word. Germany feels it has been forced to accept unreasonable terms. Poland, a part of Russia for fifty years, is made an independent country by the treaty.

German prisoners of war sink seventy German ships docked at Scapa Flow, Scotland. They say they are under orders never to surrender their warships.

There is a Communist revolt in Germany, but it is squelched.

The Fascist Party is formed by Benito Mussolini in Italy and grows rapidly.

Suggested Activities

Research: Have each student research one major event of World War I and present the information he or she finds to the class.

Cartography: Draw maps showing European boundaries before World War I and after. Also draw a map of modern-day Europe.

Read and Write: Collect firsthand accounts of the war and share them in the class as a reader's theater. Then have the students write their own accounts as though they are soldiers fighting the war or civilians caught in the middle of it.

The *Lusitania*

On Saturday, May 1, 1915, the British passenger liner *Lusitania* set sail from Pier 54 in New York, headed for Liverpool, England. On board were 1,257 passengers and 702 crew members, including the captain, William Thomas Turner. Of the passengers, 159 were Americans, and 168 were infants and children.

On board the *Lusitania* was the typical cargo carried on an ocean liner. Since the *Lusitania* was the largest passenger ship in the world, it could carry a great deal. Perhaps that is why it also carried something extra: 4,200 cases of small-caliber cartridges and other munitions.

The trip across the Atlantic was uneventful, despite the fact that New York reporters had called this the "last voyage of the *Lusitania*." War had begun nine months ago among Britain, Germany, and many other nations. There were rumors that the Germans, in their new submarines called U-boats (short for *Unterseeboot*), were likely to torpedo any enemy ship. This was, in fact, quite true. German officers had orders to sink all ships because any ship might be carrying supplies to Britain. Even passenger ships might hold food for the soldiers, and the Germans wished to stop any advantage. In the weeks prior, they had torpedoed hundreds of merchant ships in these waters.

On Friday, May 7, the *Lusitania* neared the Irish coast, and everyone was relieved to think they had sailed the ocean without incident. However, it was troubling to discover that the waters were empty. Irish ships were scheduled to escort the *Lusitania* into shore, but they were nowhere to be found. Instead, a torpedo came hurtling through the water, fired from below the surface by a German U-boat. It tore a hole in the *Lusitania*, causing it to list drastically. Many people were killed instantly. Others tried to board and release the lifeboats. The listing ship tipped back and forth, causing the lifeboats to crash against its sides. Hundreds of evacuees were thrown into the water. In 18 minutes, the *Lusitania*—which was supposed to be unsinkable—had sunk. The captain stayed until the end, eventually clinging to a floating chair for safety. The survivors of the attack held pieces of wood and other buoyant objects to keep themselves afloat. Six of the original 48 lifeboats made it safely to the water.

In all, more than 1,200 people died. Children and infants comprised about ten percent of that number, and Americans accounted for 128 of the dead.

President Wilson made a formal protest to the German government, which issued an apology for the error. However, many Americans were outraged, as were nations around the world. The sinking of the *Lusitania* became a rallying cry for troops everywhere, and eventually it became one of the catalysts for America's entry into the Great War.

Suggested Activities

Writing: Write a diary account as though you are a passenger on the *Lusitania*. Write another from the perspective of a German crewman on the attacking U-boat.

Liners: Learn about the history of passenger ships and the changes made in them from the time of the *Lusitania* to the present.

Discussion: Ask the class to discuss the roles of the British and the Germans in the *Lusitania* disaster. Were the Germans, the British, or both in the wrong?

The Last Tsar and the Red Scare

In 1900, the Russian Empire was vast and sprawling—but relatively ineffective. Revolution broke out in 1905 when workers marched to the palace of the tsar in St. Petersburg to ask for reforms. Government troops fired on the unarmed citizens, killing and wounding hundreds. Bloody Sunday, as it was known, became a catalyst for liberal leaders who were gaining in strength. Tsar Nicholas II was forced to create a *Duma*, a fully elected group of lawmakers whose purpose was to advise the tsar. However, civil unrest continued due to such events as the Russo-Japanese War of 1905 and a general strike in the same year. Revolutionaries formed a Soviet (council) called the Soviet of Workers' Duties. In response, the tsar gave the Duma power to accept or reject all laws, and this appeased some; however, revolutionary rumblings grew. The Dumas proved ineffective because the tsar would not release much power to them.

Tsar Nicholas II

War was declared on Russia in 1914 by Germany, and the resulting battles took a grave toll not only on lives but on food, fuel, and housing. Much of the Russian army was untrained, and they questioned the efficacy of the war. Soldiers in the rear did not wish to move to the front, where they would almost certainly be killed. They did not believe in or support the government of the tsar, so they had little motivation for fighting.

Nicholas was rapidly losing support. At the time, he made a variety of unwise decisions in terms of placements in top positions. Many believe that his ill-judged actions were the result of his association with Grigori Efimovich Rasputin, a "holy man" who, while saving the tsar's son from the effects of hemophilia, grew to have tremendous influence on the tsar and his wife. Rasputin was murdered by a group of nobles in 1916, but the leaders he had influenced the tsar to appoint remained in position, and so did national distrust in the tsar.

By 1917, the Russian people had grown sick of the war and the tsar's ineffectiveness. Massive revolution broke out in March. Nicholas ordered the dismantling of the Duma, but it refused and took over temporary control of the government. The tsar abdicated the throne on March 15; he, his wife, and his entire family of five children, including the *tsarevich* (heir apparent to the throne), were imprisoned.

Revolutionaries continued their battle; however, the effects of World War I had weakened them. A smaller group of revolutionaries became stronger in the face of the national chaos and confusion. In October (November by today's calendar in Russia) 1917, the Bolsheviks stormed the Winter Palace, headquarters for the temporary government, and they took control. They were directed by V. I. Lenin, who became Russia's new leader. Lenin completely withdrew Russia from World War I, took over Russia's industries, seized most of the nation's farm products, and changed the name of the Labor Party to the Russian Communist Party.

Tsar Nicholas and his family disappeared in Siberia in 1918. It was believed that Bolshevik revolutionaries killed the tsar and his family and secretly buried the bodies.

The Last Tsar and the Red Scare *(cont.)*

Meanwhile, in the United States in 1919, the "Red Scare" stormed across the nation. On April 28, a package containing a bomb was delivered to the home of Senator Thomas Hartwick, badly injuring his maid. In June, another bomb was sent to Attorney General A. Mitchell Palmer. Panic swept throughout the nation, and 6,000 people (primarily foreigners) were arrested for attempting to overthrow the government. Almost none were convicted. However, suspicion of immigrants who did not speak English—or whose ancestors did not speak English—continued to grow. Individuals with political opinions that differed from the norm were suspected of being Russian spies. They were called "radicals" and were ostracized.

Civil war continued in Russia from 1918 through 1920 between the Communists and the anti-Communists. The Communists won, and in 1922 they created a new nation, the Union of Soviet Socialist Republics (U.S.S.R.). The U.S.S.R. would remain intact for seventy years until its eventual dissolution in 1991.

Suggested Activities

Research: Find out more about the leadership of Tsar Nicholas II and the influence of Rasputin.

Cartography: Draw a map of the Russian Empire circa 1900 and another circa 1922. How do they differ? Also draw a modern map of Russia. How is it different now?

Politics and History: Report on the political history between the United States and Russia from 1900 to the present. How have diplomatic ties been strained and how have they been strengthened?

Prominent People: Research the lives of some prominent people involved in the Russian Revolution. Names include V. I. Lenin, Alexander Kerensky, Grigori Rasputin, Tsar Nicholas II, Joseph Stalin, Karl Marx, and others.

A Mystery: Anna Anderson, who died in Charlottesville, Virginia, in 1984, claimed for 40 years that she was Nicholas II's youngest daughter, the Grand Duchess Anastasia. In the 1950s, the film *Anastasia*, starring Ingrid Bergman, told a fictionalized version of this story. In 1989, scientific tests done on remains found in a mass grave in Siberia in 1979 proved them to be those of the tsar, the tsarina, three daughters, and four followers. Alexis, heir to the throne, and one daughter, both known to have been in the royal party, were missing. Research Anna Anderson's claims, the reaction of related royalty, and the role of modern science in establishing the truth. Was she really a Romanov? What do you think happened to the children missing from the grave?

Rasputin: Rasputin proved hard for the Russians to kill. Three attempts were made before they were finally successful. Find out what they tried and how they eventually did away with the "holy man" whom they believed to be an influence of evil.

Bolsheviks: Learn about what the Bolsheviks stood for and the kind of government they were interested in developing.

Revolutions: Have the students compare and contrast, either in writing or orally, the American Revolution and the Russian Revolution.

Women Legislators

Nellie Letitia McClung was born in Chatsworth, Ontario, Canada, in 1873. Seven years later, Jeannette Rankin was born near Missoula, Montana. Neither woman knew the other during her lifetime; however, they were separately fighting similar battles in their neighboring nations.

Nellie McClung was a leading political reformer in Canada in the early twentieth century. In 1912, she helped to form the Winnipeg Political Equality League, founded to help win suffrage for women. In 1916, the League proved successful, and the right to vote was granted to the women of Manitoba (the province in which Winnipeg is located). Two years later, all of Canada's women had the right to vote.

McClung also served on the legislature of the province of Alberta from 1921 to 1926. In 1927, she and four other women fought a groundbreaking battle in court over whether or not women were considered "persons" under the British North America Act, Canada's Constitution of the time. They won their case in 1929, allowing women in Canada to serve on the nation's Senate. McClung was truly a legislative reformer.

Nellie Letitia McClung

Jeannette Rankin

Another such reformer was Jeannette Rankin, who, at the same time as McClung, was fighting a legislative battle in America. Also like McClung, Rankin won. In 1914, Rankin led a campaign in her home state of Montana to give women the vote. She was victorious. Her campaign included riding back and forth across her state on horseback, talking to as many people as she could. In 1916, she was elected by the people of Montana to serve in the United States House of Representatives as a Congresswoman at large. As such, she became the first woman elected to the United States Congress. In 1940, Rankin was again elected to the House of Representatives for a single term. While in Congress, she voted against United States participation in World War I, and she was the only member of the House to vote against U.S. participation in World War II. In her later years, Rankin opposed U.S. participation in the Korean War and the Vietnam War.

Nellie McClung died in 1951, and Jeannette Rankin died in 1973. However, the memorable legacies of the two women live on.

Suggested Activities

Women in Politics: Learn about other notable women in U.S. and Canadian politics. What have been their contributions? Pay particular attention to the women serving today.

Suffrage: Trace the history of suffrage for women around the world. How have the battles differed and how have they been the same? What people—men and women—helped to bring the right to vote for women?

New Mexico and Arizona

In 1911, there were 46 states within the United States, but by early 1912, that number had increased by two. On January 6, 1912, New Mexico joined the Union; a few weeks later, on February 14, Arizona entered as the forty-eighth state. Arizona would remain the youngest state until 1959, when Alaska and Hawaii were admitted.

New Mexico and Arizona are well known for their beautiful scenery and multicultural heritage. Today, they retain much of the influence of their Native American and Spanish ancestries as well as the nineteenth-century sense of the Old West. Many tourists are drawn to the states' colorful deserts and mountains and strong senses of history and culture. Perhaps best known in the area is the Grand Canyon of Arizona, which brings millions of visitors annually from around the world.

However, this reverence for the area has not always been present. New Mexico had hoped for more than 60 years to become a state; however, it is believed that strong prejudices against its primarily Spanish-speaking, Catholic population kept the territory's attempts unsuccessful. All of that changed during President Taft's administration, and in 1910, New Mexico was allowed to draft its constitution. In 1912, it became the forty-seventh state.

With statehood, New Mexican economy and tourism immediately began to flourish. The Native American cultures, including their ceremonies and arts, were significant draws to U.S. citizens and others from around the world. Also, the dry climate of the area was considered by many to promote a robust health, so thousands came, hoping to be made well.

Arizona tried as early as 1877 to be accepted as a state, but had no success. Congress attempted in 1904 and 1906 to confer statehood upon the areas of New Mexico and Arizona as one state; however, Arizona balked at the idea. In 1911, Congress resolved to allow statehood for Arizona, but President Taft vetoed the resolution because the proposed constitution allowed voters to recall state judges. When Arizona's voters removed that provision from the constitution, Arizona was made a state. A few months later, the voters reinstated the recall into the state constitution.

Over the course of the past century, Arizona has changed from its early days of mining and cattle raising to all the modern industry and business that the rest of the nation enjoys; yet, the state still captures the feel of the Old West for the sake of tourism as well as history.

Suggested Activities

Sequence: Research to find the order in which each of the 50 U.S. states joined the Union. On a large map, attach numbers with sticky notes, designating the order. Then discuss the possibility of future states being added to the union.

Geography: Study the geography of the southwestern United States, particularly Arizona and New Mexico. Discuss why the states are such significant tourist draws.

Health: Many people still come to Arizona and New Mexico for reasons of health. Research to find out why the states' climates help some individuals.

Report: Write a report about either New Mexico or Arizona. Include these topics: its capital, area, and population; state motto, bird, flower, tree, and song; important physical features; industry and economy; culture; geography; history.

The Sixteenth and Seventeenth Amendments

The Constitution of the United States is the supreme law of the land. First ratified in 1789, it was accepted by all thirteen states by May 29, 1790. It was immediately followed with ten amendments which were drafted by the First Congress, and these amendments became known as the Bill of Rights.

Other amendments followed the first ten over the course of the next century. The 1910s saw the ratification of two of those amendments, the sixteenth and seventeenth. They are as follows:

Amendment 16 *(ratified February 3, 1913)*

The Congress shall have the power to lay and collect taxes on incomes, from whatever source derived, without apportionment among the several States, and without regard to any census or enumeration.

Amendment 17 *(ratified April 8, 1913)*

The Senate of the United States shall be composed of two Senators from each State, elected by the people thereof for six years; and each Senator shall have one vote. The electors in each State shall have the qualifications requisite for electors of the most numerous branch of the State legislatures.

When vacancies happen in the representation of any State in the Senate, the executive authority of such State shall issue writs of election to fill such vacancies. Provided, That the legislature of any State may empower the executive thereof to make temporary appointments until the people fill the vacancies by election as the legislature may direct.

This amendment shall not be so construed as to affect the election or term of any Senator chosen before it becomes valid as part of the Constitution.

The Sixteenth Amendment came as a result of a Supreme Court decision that a federal tax on income gained through property and not divided and allotted among the states was unconstitutional. This amendment allowed Congress to levy taxes on income derived from any source.

The Seventeenth Amendment came about through popular demand over a long period of time. The citizens of the United States wanted to elect Senators through popular vote, and this amendment allowed them to do just that.

Suggested Activities

What Do They Mean?: Legal language can be difficult to understand. People study the law for years in order to interpret its meaning! Challenge yourself to understand the language of these amendments by translating them into everyday language. Use a dictionary and thesaurus to help you.

History: Learn about the Constitution, its creators, and other documents upon which it may have been based. Find out why the information included in the Bill of Rights was not part of the original Constitution.

William Howard Taft

27th President, 1909–1913

Vice President: James S. Sherman
Born: September 15, 1857, in Cincinnati, Ohio
Died: March 8, 1930
Party: Republican
Parents: Alphonso Taft, Louise Maria Torrey
First Lady: Helen Herron
Children: Robert, Helen, Charles
Nickname: Big Bill
Education: Yale College and Cincinnati Law School
Famous Firsts:

- Taft was the first president to serve on the Supreme Court.
- He was the first to protect federal lands on which oil had been found.
- He bought the first cars used at the White House, and he built the first garage for their storage.
- Taft was the first president to throw out the first ball on the opening day of the baseball season.
- Always large, Taft was the heaviest president ever, weighing 332 pounds at his inauguration.
- Under President McKinley's appointment, he became the first commissioner of the Philippines, a holding the United States won from Spain in 1900.
- He was the first president to be buried at Arlington National Cemetery. The only other president buried there is John F. Kennedy.

Achievements:

- He took steps toward establishing a federal budget by having his cabinet members submit reports of their needs. It was estimated that he saved the nation $42 million in 1910.
- Taft actualized many of Teddy Roosevelt's programs by working them into law during his presidency.
- He was very successful in protecting federal lands set aside for conservation. In fact, he was even more successful than Roosevelt, whose name is usually linked with conservation.
- Taft oversaw twice as many prosecutions under the Sherman Antitrust Act than did Roosevelt. Most impressively, Taft succeeded in breaking up the Standard Oil Company monopoly.
- The Sixteenth and Seventeenth Amendments were passed while Taft was in office.
- New Mexico and Arizona became states during his presidency.
- After the presidency, Taft became a law professor at Yale, the president of the American Bar Association, chairman of the National War Labor Board, and Chief Justice of the United States.

Interesting Facts:

- Taft never really wanted to be president. His desire was to serve on the Supreme Court.
- Due to Taft's size, a new bathtub had to be placed in the White House. It could hold four average-sized adults.
- Taft was often criticized for playing golf, which was considered to be a rich man's game. However, he played while conducting business with important leaders, a fact that the newspapers never reported.
- The president was most criticized because of his differences with Teddy Roosevelt. Although Roosevelt had handpicked Taft as his successor, he later changed his mind when he saw that Taft was more conservative than he liked. Taft had also changed members of Roosevelt's old cabinet, although Roosevelt had promised them they could keep their positions. Taft was deeply hurt by Roosevelt's rejection. Roosevelt had been his mentor. The strife between the two split the Republican party and made the way easier for a Democratic president in the next election.

Woodrow Wilson

28th President, 1913–1921

Vice President: Thomas R. Marshall

Born: December 29, 1856, in Stanton, Virginia

Died: February 23, 1924

Party: Democrat

Parents: Joseph Ruggles, Jessie Janet Woodrow

First Ladies: Ellen Louise Axson, Edith Bolling Galt

Children: Margaret, Jessie, Eleanor

Nickname: Professor

Education: Ph.D.

Famous Firsts:

- Wilson was the first president to hold a press conference.
- He was the most educated president and the first with a Ph.D.
- Wilson was the first president to travel to Europe.
- He was the first to be widowed and then to marry while in office.

Achievements:

- With the ratification of the Sixteenth Amendment, income tax became legal. The Federal Reserve Act was instituted; this agency controlled the money supply.
- In 1917, he was forced to declare war against Germany. For three years, he had been able to maintain U.S. neutrality in the Great War.
- On January 8, 1918, Wilson presented his Fourteen Points for peace.
- He negotiated the Treaty of Versailles, which also established the League of Nations.
- For his work in ending World War I, Wilson was awarded the Nobel Peace Prize.

Interesting Facts:

- After suffering a stroke, Wilson allowed his wife to handle lesser government details. She decided which matters were important enough to bring to his attention.
- Wilson typed his own letters on a typewriter that could type in either English or Greek.
- He did not have an inaugural ball because he considered them to be frivolous.
- Wilson's second wife, Edith, was a descendent of Pocahontas.
- Two of Wilson's three daughters were married at the White House.
- The Wilsons kept a flock of sheep on the White House lawn to keep the grass trimmed. After the lambs' wool was sheared, it was sold and the money was donated to the Red Cross.
- Edith Wilson spent a great deal of time sewing for the Red Cross during the time that the United States fought in World War I.
- His original given name was Thomas Woodrow, and as a child he was known as Tommy. He stopped using this name after college.

New Freedom Legislation

President Wilson spearheaded a variety of legislation under his campaign promise of a "New Freedom," which he declared would free American potential rather than control it. Voters accepted his promise, and once elected, Wilson kept the promise with the following legislation and agencies:

Federal Reserve System

The Federal Reserve System (FRS) was created in 1914 to manage the nation's banks, to make credit easier to get, and to stimulate economic activity. The FRS became a bank for the populous as well as for the government. Its primary role today is in stabilizing the banking system of the nation.

Federal Trade Commission

The Federal Trade Commission (FTC) was created in 1914 to prevent monopolies, the control of an industry by one company or group of companies. Monopolies can force prices to rise artificially because of their blanket control of an industry. The FTC has the ability to stop companies from entering into such illegal activities.

Clayton Antitrust Act

This act was created to halt monopolies and to prevent them from being used against labor unions.

Federal Farm Loan Act and Warehouse Act

These acts were intended to help farmers get loans.

Adamson Act

This act set a workday of eight hours for interstate railroad workers.

Despite the advances made by Wilson and his administration, there were limitations to his "New Freedom." An industrial decline followed by war (and therefore disruption in foreign trade) provided little economic help, and Wilson glaringly neglected to honor his campaign promise of fairness to blacks. Under pressure from his fellow Southerners, Wilson allowed racial segregation in federal government offices. He supported the segregation by saying that it was in the best interest of blacks.

Suggested Activities

Research: Choose either the Federal Reserve System or the Federal Trade Commission and research to find out more about its history and activities. Share your findings with the class.

Success: Was Wilson a successful president? Learn more about his successes and failures, then hold a class debate to determine whether or not Wilson was a successful leader.

Monopoly: Play the popular game Monopoly to see firsthand how monopolies work. Discuss the results.

Segregation: Racial segregation was a part of American politics, economics, culture, and society for many years. Learn about the history of segregation and how it came to end.

First Lady: Wilson's second wife, Edith, took a strong leadership role during Wilson's last months as president. After suffering a stroke, Wilson was too weak to lead on his own. Edith decided which matters were significant enough to bring to his attention. Research to learn more about Edith Wilson and her role in the presidency.

Fourteen Points

On January 8, 1918, President Woodrow Wilson made a speech to Congress. In it, he outlined fourteen points for peace and prosperity in the world after the war. The son of a Presbyterian minister, Wilson often took a moral stance in his politics, believing the role of the president was to lead the moral direction of the nation. Wilson's plan, which was called the Fourteen Points, was part of his overall plan to do just that.

Wilson also wished to build the morale of the Allies, weary and embittered from the long war. Likewise, the Central Powers needed to be appeased and assured of just treatment despite their losses. In presenting his ideas, Wilson said, "We demand that the world be made fit and safe to live in . . . against force and selfish aggression. The program of the world's peace is our only program." He also declared that the Fourteen Points were "the moral climax of the final war for liberty."

The Fourteen Points that Wilson outlined are as follows:

1. No secret diplomacy
2. Freedom of the seas in both peace and war
3. Removal of international barriers to trade; international establishment of equal trade conditions
4. Arms reductions around the world
5. Impartial adjustment of all colonial claims
6. No foreign interference in Russian affairs
7. Complete Belgian sovereignty
8. Alsace-Lorraine returned to France
9. Equitable redrawing of Italian boundaries for all internal nationalities
10. Autonomous development in Austria-Hungary of all internal nationalities (self-determination)
11. Serbian access to the sea; restoration of the Balkan nations
12. Sovereignty for the Turkish parts of the Ottoman Empire
13. Independence for Poland and access to the sea
14. Formation of an independent body of arbitration or League of Nations (see page 26)

On the night of October 3, 1918, after their massive offensive had failed, the Germans sent a note to President Wilson. In it, they called for a truce and negotiations based on Wilson's Fourteen Points.

When he made his proposal to Congress, Wilson did not offer any details about how to make the plan work; nonetheless, he received enormous public support for his ideas. However, the council at the Paris Peace Conference of 1919 did present a great deal of opposition. Wilson was forced to modify his ideas and to make compromises while negotiating the peace treaties.

━━━━━━ Suggested Activity ━━━━━━

Peace: Have the students write their own proposals for world peace.

The League of Nations

The final point of President Wilson's Fourteen Points plan was the formation of a League of Nations. In Paris, Wilson outlined a plan for the League. He said that it would be an international organization, the purpose of which was to preserve peace throughout the world. Every nation in the world would be a member, and each nation would have an equal vote. Any controversy within the League would be turned over to the Central Council. The Council would consist of France, Britain, Italy, Japan, the United States, and five small nations. It would serve as arbiter to these controversies and would propose peaceful and fair solutions. Any nations which refused to accept the decision of the Council would suffer economic sanctions and, perhaps, incur military action. Wilson told the Allies that peace depended "upon one great force . . . the moral force of the public opinion of the world."

After great debate, the diplomats agreed to the tenets of the treaty, accepting the League of Nations. Wilson returned to the United States after negotiating the treaty in Europe for six months. Meanwhile, his health had begun to fail him, and his influence with Congress had diminished during his long absence. Upon his return, he discovered that Congressional response to the tenets of the treaty was not altogether favorable. A group of 39 Republican senators—led by Henry Cabot Lodge—opposed the League of Nations, citing several flaws in its structure. These flaws included the lack of procedures for members to withdraw from the League, the failure of the League to recognize the Monroe Doctrine, and the ability of the Central Council to disregard the internal affairs of a nation when the Council makes a decision regarding that nation.

Wilson and the Republicans were at odds. For the president, the League of Nations was the most important component of the treaty. However, the Senators in opposition believed that the United States should remain "isolationist," staying out of international affairs. They wanted the League of Nations dropped from the treaty.

Wilson went on a national campaign to garner support for the League. However, after three weeks of exhaustive traveling and speaking, he physically broke down; upon his return to Washington, he suffered a stroke. While he was recuperating, he refused to renegotiate the treaty. The Senate defeated it in March of 1920.

Of course, the Allies had already agreed to the treaty, and the League went on without the United States, although not so soundly. The terms of the treaty, however, were never acceptable to the Germans, and the vast economic burdens placed on them paved the way for the rise of Adolf Hitler just a decade or so later. The ineffective League of Nations would be powerless to stop the growing crisis, and Wilson's Fourteen Points were all but wasted.

Suggested Activities

History: Find out what happened to the League of Nations in the years following the Treaty of Versailles. Also, research the United Nations and its relationship to the League.

The First Lady: During the end of his presidency, Wilson's wife Edith managed a number of his affairs, deciding for herself which matters needed to be brought before the president. Find out more about her role during this critical period in U.S. history.

Election Facts and Figures

	Election of 1908	Election of 1912	Election of 1916
Democrats	William Jennings Bryan of Nebraska made his third attempt at the presidency on the Democratic ticket. John W. Kern, a Democratic leader from Indiana, was his running mate.	Governor Woodrow Wilson of New Jersey was the nominee, and Governor Thomas R. Marshall of Indiana was his running mate.	Wilson was easily renominated. Marshall remained his running mate.
Republicans	William Howard Taft was Theodore Roosevelt's choice for his successor. James S. Sherman, a Congressman from New York, was Taft's running mate.	Former President Roosevelt decided to run again. His opposition to Taft split the party, but Taft got the nomination.	Justice Charles Evans Hughes of the Supreme Court became the nominee.
Other	No other major candidates surfaced during this election.	Roosevelt ran under the Progressive "Bull Moose" Party with Senator Hiram W. Johnson of California.	No other major candidates surfaced during this election.
Issues	Government corruption and unfair business practices were major issues. Bryan was a supporter of income tax, prohibition, and women's suffrage. All his causes eventually became law.	Checks on big business, honest government, conservation, and social justice were the issues.	At issue were the Great War, child labor, laws for workers, and women's suffrage.
Slogans	Taft campaigned as "Bill."	"New Nationalism" was a phrase coined by Roosevelt to represent the issues. He also talked about giving everyone a "Square Deal." Wilson's platform was called the "New Freedom."	Wilson's campaign slogan was "He kept us out of war."
Results	Taft took 321 electoral votes to Bryan's 162.	The split in the Republican party helped to bring about a Democratic win. Wilson took 435 electoral votes, Roosevelt took 88, and the incumbent president, Taft, took only 8.	Wilson won, but narrowly. Had California voted Republican, Hughes would have been elected. The final electoral vote was Wilson 277, Hughes 254.

More About the Elections

Here are some ways to use the Election Facts and Figures on page 27. Select those activities and projects which best suit your classroom needs.

1. Prepare a classroom chart with two different sections, each marked with a vice president's name from the 1910s. Pair the students. Allow each pair to select (or randomly give them) a vice president's name. Instruct the pairs to find out more about the men nominated for vice president: where they were born, their childhoods and schooling, their political backgrounds, what became of them after office, and so forth. Compile all the information gathered onto your prepared chart.

2. President Wilson won very narrowly in the campaign of 1916. Research as a class to determine the reasons why the election was so close.

3. Percentages of electoral votes occasionally do not reflect the percentages of popular votes. Have the students study the electoral system to determine how it works. They can then take sides in a debate over this system of electing a president.

4. Former President Theodore Roosevelt played a significant role in the defeat of incumbent President Taft in the election of 1912. Learn about the history between Taft and Roosevelt and how Roosevelt turned the tide of the election.

5. The "New Nationalism" and the "New Freedom" became important terms in the election of 1912. Do some research to determine what these terms mean, why they were important, and the effects they had on the elections.

6. In the election of 1916, the fact that Wilson had kept the nation out of war was important to his being re-elected. However, within a short period of time, the U.S. declared war on Germany. Find out what happened from 1916 to 1917 to change Wilson's stance on America's participation in the war. How did the American people respond to this change?

7. Throughout the first decade of the 20th century, Republicans held the presidency. In 1913, Democrats came into power and stayed until 1921. What affect did this have on the nation? Compare this period of time to other times in American history that have been dominated by the Republicans or Democrats over a space of about a decade or more.

8. Extend the information provided on page 27 with other facts and figures. For example, find out how many popular votes the candidates garnered in their respective elections. Make a chart comparing the figures. See page 29 for some math problems that use these figures.

9. Woodrow Wilson was influential in bringing about peace from war, and in 1919, he was awarded the Nobel Prize for peace. Research to find why this was so.

10. Roosevelt ran in 1912 under the Progressive "Bull Moose" Party. Find out about this party, what it stood for, and how it came to be.

Election Math

In the chart below, you will find the number of electoral votes and popular votes for each presidential election of the 1910s (including the election of 1908). Use this chart to answer the questions that follow. Show your work.

Year	Candidate	Electoral Vote	Popular Vote
1908	Bryan	162	6,412,294
	Taft	321	7,675,320
1912	Wilson	435	6,286,214
	Taft	8	3,483,922
	Roosevelt	88	4,216,020
1916	Wilson	277	9,129,606
	Hughes	254	8,538,221

1. How many more electoral votes were there in 1912 than in 1908?

2. How many popular votes were there altogether in 1916?

3. How many total electoral votes votes were there in all three elections?

4. Using the figure from problem #3, what is the average number of electoral votes per election?

5. Using the answer from problem #4, which actual number of electoral votes (total from one election) comes closest to the average number?

6. What is the combined number of popular votes that Wilson received in his two elections?

7. What percentage of popular votes did Roosevelt receive in 1912? (Round the answer.)

8. What percentage of electoral votes did Roosevelt receive in 1912? (Round the answer.)

Triangle Shirtwaist Company

Immigration reached its peak in the first 20 years of the century. In that time, countless immigrants took low-paying jobs with poor working conditions simply to make money to survive. They had no other choice. However, workers were becoming increasingly vocal about the work environment and low wages, and strikes were commonplace—although controversial—occurrences.

In February of 1910, the employees of 13 firms in New York City held a strike for better conditions. The strike proved unsuccessful, and their demands were denied. One of these firms was the Triangle Shirtwaist Company on Greene Street.

March 25, 1911, was payday at Triangle, and it was almost quitting time. On the tenth floor, paychecks had been distributed to the many workers, most of whom were Jewish and Italian immigrant girls. Suddenly and without warning, a raging fire broke out and swept through the floor. The one available escape route could not possibly let all the employees pass. Very few escaped. The others either burned or leapt to their deaths out the tenth-floor window, still clutching their paychecks. In all, 146 young girls and women died.

Although the building had been proclaimed fireproof by the city fire inspectors, it had no sprinkler system and only one exit. A second exit was bolted shut. According to the surviving workers, the second door was fastened to keep employees from stealing spools of thread. However, due to the recent strikes and labor unrest, it was believed by many that the door was bolted to keep outside labor agitators from getting inside to incite the workers.

The tragedy at Triangle drew the attention of the nation, horrified at the needless deaths. News of the fire also brought to light many of the poor conditions under which the girls had worked. Therefore, the lives of the girls were not lost in vain, because their tragedy helped build momentum for improved labor laws and working conditions.

Suggested Activities

Sweat Shops: The Triangle Shirtwaist Company was one of many sweatshops in big cities such as New York. Find out more about sweatshops and the working conditions there.

Immigration: New York was a center for immigration throughout the late 19th and early 20th centuries. Learn more about the patterns of immigration at the time, where people came from, and why they came to America. This research should lead to an understanding of why many were willing to tolerate the poor working conditions of sweatshops and other businesses.

30

Child Labor

By 1911, there were more than two million children working in the United States, most of them in unhealthy and unsafe conditions for very little compensation. These were the children of the poor and new immigrants who worked to help provide basic needs for the family. However, they also worked because the growing American economy called for cheap, mass labor to produce its expanding base of commerce. Children as young as six worked in coal mines, garment factories, and other industries, keeping up with American demands.

Although the general populace was aware that children were regularly employed to support industry, most people turned a blind eye to the labor conditions in which they worked. No one really wanted to consider what daily life was like for these children. However, from 1911 through 1916, all of that changed with the National Child Labor Committee (NCLC) and a photographer named Lewis Wickes Hine.

Hine was employed by the NCLC to photograph children at work in the exploitative and unsafe conditions they knew to exist. For five years, Hine used whatever means available to gain access to the Southern and Eastern industries where children were being used exploitatively. In order to gain access to the factories, he pretended to be an insurance agent, a fire inspector, an industrial photographer, and even a Bible salesman. Sometimes he used a hidden camera because, understandably, employers were not eager to have the factory conditions for children photographed. Whenever Hine was barred from a business, he photographed the children entering and leaving—dirty, sad, and often in pain.

Through Hine's photographs, which were published in many of the most popular magazines of the day, the NCLC was able to gain enormous public support for its cause. People were no longer able to remain in denial about the exploitation of children in industry. They saw the photos of bedraggled, soot-covered breaker boys who stooped through ten- and twelve-hour days to separate rock from coal. They saw the photos of young girls standing over large sewing machines to change bobbins, in terrible danger of their hair or a finger being caught in the machinery. There were even photos of children who had lost limbs in the dangerous equipment.

In 1916, the work of the NCLC seemed to be successful with the passage of the Keating-Owen Act, banning the interstate sale of items produced by child labor. However, two years later the Supreme Court ruled the act unconstitutional.

Conditions for and restrictions on child labor did not come into effect until 1938 when the Fair Labor Standards were passed, establishing a minimum wage and limiting the age of child workers to 16 and over (18 and over for hazardous occupations). Children 14 and over were allowed to work in certain after-school occupations.

It is important to note, however, that children still labor in certain industries, particularly migrant children in agriculture, and many products sold in the United States are produced by child laborers overseas. However, just as the NCLC and Lewis Wickes Hine did in the 1910s, reformers today are working hard to bring unsafe and unfair practices in child labor to the public's attention.

Suggested Activities

History: Trace the history of child labor in the United States. Also, chart those industries that regularly employ children today—for example, the entertainment industry. Under what conditions do children work in such modern industries?

Labor Reform

The 1910s were important times for laborers who were fighting for improved labor practices, including working conditions, wages, workday length, and the limiting of child labor. A number of unions and labor leaders came to the forefront, and labor was an important issue during every presidential campaign. Here are some of the major labor-related events of the 1910s.

1910 Frederick W. Taylor, the self-proclaimed "father of scientific management," put forth a scientific approach to work. Taylor observed workers everywhere and outlined for businesses precise ways to curb "excess" time. Businesses hailed the engineer; laborers condemned him.

1912 50,000 workers in the textile mill industry of Lawrence, Massachusetts, began to strike in January. The strikers, who represented 28 nationalities, were seeking increased wages. When legislation reduced the work week to 54 hours from 56 for women and children, the wool and cotton mill workers saw their paychecks cut. During the strike, which sometimes turned violent, two workers were killed. Business leaders blamed the strike on civil unrest in foreign nations. The strikers were backed by the Industrial Workers of the World, a powerful labor union.

1913 A New Jersey strike was lost by the Industrial Workers of the World after the arrests of many strikers, which broke the workers' morale.

Striking mine workers in Ludlow, Colorado, were killed by National Guardsmen who said they were simply trying to restore order in the face of near anarchy. The dead included three men, two women, and thirteen children.

A battle over labor in Butte, Montana, ended with the complete dismantling of the thirty-six-year-old union, the Western Federation of Miners. The Union lost support when it failed to protect hundreds of fired workers. The state militia was required to keep the peace in Butte.

1914 With the new Clayton Antitrust Act, Congress gave organized labor the right to strike, to boycott, and to picket peacefully. Prior to this time, unions could be prosecuted for striking. The act also outlawed a number of corrupt business practices.

1916 In 1916, there were 1.8 million child laborers in the United States. The Keating-Owen Act, a federal child labor law, was passed in that year, banning interstate commerce of products made by children under 14 years of age. Also, children under age 16 were banned from working in mines, working at night, and working more than eight hours per day. Southerners in the cotton-producing states were the most opposed to this new legislation (see page 31).

1918 One million women were working in factories due to the war overseas in which millions of men were fighting. However, many labor unions would not accept the women or help them to receive fair treatment. The women were universally paid less than the men had been.

1919 350,000 steel workers held a strike for three months. The strike was often violent and resulted in 20 deaths. The workers demanded union recognition, an eight-hour workday, and the end of 24-hour shifts. Though their efforts failed, their solidarity helped to strengthen organized labor everywhere.

An International Labor Conference in Washington endorsed an eight-hour workday.

Suggested Activities

People: Mary Harris "Mother" Jones, William "Big Bill" Haywood, William Z. Foster, Blackie Ford, and Joseph Ettor were just some of the important labor leaders of the time. Eugene Debs was also noteworthy as a socialist and supporter of the working-class individual. Find out about these labor leaders, what they did, and why labor laws were so important to them.

Today: Follow a current strike or boycott. Report to the class on the details and results.

Assembly Lines

The assembly-line system in industry is a relatively simple one and is in common use today, but it was not until 1913, under the direction of Henry Ford, that it really came into widespread practice.

An assembly line is an arrangement in a factory whereby the work that must be done to complete a product is passed progressively from one employee or station to the next. Each individual, team, or machine specializes in one aspect of the overall production and completes that one task or group of tasks repeatedly throughout the business day as each item comes to the station ready for the necessary work.

Henry Ford

At the dawn of the twentieth century, the factory system was the standard mode of production in industry. However, assembly-line techniques forever changed factory operations. A mechanic named Ransom Eli Olds first used the assembly line in his automobile factory, the Olds Motor Vehicle Company, in 1897. (Olds went on to produce one of the most popular cars of the 1920s, the Reo.) However, it is Henry Ford who is most often credited with the creation of the assembly line, and truly it was the latter manufacturer who brought it into the industrial consciousness. Through Ford's work, the assembly line became adopted as the standard for industrial work. His factories are largely responsible for the enormous expansion of American industry and, consequently, the rise in the standard of living.

Ford used standardized, interchangeable parts in his assembly lines, and immediately his production skyrocketed. However, employee turnover also jumped significantly. There was a monthly turnover of forty to sixty percent of the employees because workers became bored with the redundancy of the work and the increased quotas were more than they were willing to meet. Ford countered this challenge with increased wages, doubling them from about $2.50 to $5.00 per day. The rapid turnovers began to level off while operating costs reduced dramatically through the use of the assembly lines. Furthermore, industrial output increased, and the profits that were seen in 1913 had doubled just three years later. Modern industry was born.

One significant aspect of the factory and assembly-line systems that is important to note is how they served to promote the employment of women. Factories were one of the earliest emancipators of women, allowing them wage-earning opportunities and financial independence. During wartime, women flocked to the factories and were critical in keeping them operational.

Today, the techniques of the 1910s have been greatly modernized. Technology has replaced numerous employees. Of course, individuals are still needed to operate and create the technology.

However, automation has definitely become the way of the future, doing for modern industry what Ford and the assembly line did in 1913.

Suggested Activity

Do It Yourself: Create a classroom assembly line for the creation of any product, from the making of a recipe to an art project to a paper airplane. Make comparisons between the individual creation of such a product and its creation through an assembly line. Which is more expeditious? Which has the greater quality? Which has greater perceived value? Discuss your findings as a class.

Selective Service

When war in Europe broke out, the people in the United States strongly supported the Allies (although many immigrants of German descent stood in favor of the Central Powers). The U.S. government felt secure that, should they join the war, millions of young men would voluntarily enlist. There was a common belief at the time that dying for one's country was a noble and valiant act.

The United States managed to retain a neutral position in the war for three years, but growing hostilities and antagonism drove the United States to declare war in 1917. Immediately, millions of men enlisted. Patriotism, the threat of German victory, and Uncle Sam all persuaded them to fight. As President Wilson said, "The world must be made safe for democracy," and the young men agreed.

Around the nation, recruiting posters could be seen, bearing the now famous image of Uncle Sam calling for American support. An artist named James Montgomery Flagg painted the image. The Army added the words "I Want You [for the] U.S. Army." Millions answered the call.

The president and Secretary of War Newton D. Baker felt confident that these recruitment tactics would be enough to build a strong army. Others believed that the numbers of enlisted men would need to be supplemented with draftees. The draft is a process of selecting individuals for military service. Certain individuals are excluded for health and other reasons. Those that are acceptable are chosen in random fashion. They must then join the armed services, regardless of their desire to do so.

Throughout the length of the Great War, Americans debated the value of the draft. Many believed that it was the best way to strengthen the military. Others felt that individual freedom of choice should never be taken away, and they opposed it for humanitarian reasons. Their critics said that racism was the only reason the opponents of the draft did not want it since they would have to fight alongside members of races they did not like.

In February of 1917, President Wilson and Mr. Baker reversed their positions on the draft. They authorized the Selective Service Act, a bill mandating draft registration for every able young man of suitable age. Congress then approved the act and made it law. The Selective Service System, headed by Provost Marshal General Enoch H. Crowder, was now in effect.

Suggested Activities

Drawing: Have the students design and draw recruiting posters.

Discussion: As a class, discuss the draft and students' opinions of it.

Kindergartens

Kindergarten means "children's garden" in German. Friedrich Frobel established the first kindergarten in Blankenburg, Germany, in 1837. His purpose was to support young children in developing freely, and he wanted to teach them about the nature of God. One of Frobel's pupils, Margaretha Meyer Schurz, began the first American kindergarten. Word of mouth spread the popularity of her school. Public kindergartens began to appear in the United States and Canada in the 1870s, and their purpose was primarily educational. Slowly, the movement grew.

By the turn of the century, kindergartens could be found in most large cities. However, it was not until the second decade of the new century that they spread like wildfire. Suddenly, kindergartens were everywhere, and they were extremely popular. Had their popularity diminished, they would today be called a fad of the 1910s.

Suggested Activity

Investigation: Arrange to visit a modern kindergarten. While there, observe what you see and answer the questions below. Then, research to find answers to the same questions for a kindergarten circa 1915. How do the modern and earlier kindergartens compare?

	Modern	Earlier
How many children are in the class?		
How many teachers are there?		
What are the main activities the children do?		
Using your best reasoning, what is the purpose of this kindergarten?		

Jack Johnson and the Great White Hope

Teacher Note: The subject matter of this story in history is controversial and likely to spark some heated discussion. Use your own discretion.

One of the great athletes of the early twentieth century was a champion boxer, Jack Johnson. Johnson is also noteworthy as a groundbreaker in the sport, and, indeed, in American society.

On December 26, 1908, a fight took place in Sydney, Australia, between world heavyweight boxing champion Tommy Burns, a white man, and an up-and-coming boxer, Jack Johnson, who was black. White fans were stunned when Johnson won the match. Racism was strong at the time, and many whites believed they belonged to a superior race. After Johnson won, they called for "the great white hope," a white boxer to beat the black man. Whites were further angered by Johnson because they felt he was overly confident and even arrogant in his attitude. He knew he was talented, and he was not afraid to say so. Matters were complicated when Johnson married two times, each time to a white woman. For racist whites, this was unacceptable and Johnson needed to be "put down."

Johnson's most famous fight came on Independence Day of 1910. Both the public's cry for a white fighter to beat the black champion and the lure of a healthy cash reward, encouraged thirty-five-year-old former champion Jim Jeffries to come out of retirement after five years. The public was sure he would put the "upstart" in his place. In a grueling 15-round match in Reno, Nevada, Jeffries fought relentlessly, despite the beating he received, and Johnson fought with full power, despite the deep cut he sustained over his right eye in the sixth round. Johnson, ever confident, was heard to say during the match, "I thought this fellow could hit." Johnson beat Jeffries, winning by a knockout, to maintain his title.

After the match, racist sentiment caused a series of riots across the country. In all, eight black people were killed in the rioting. One man was simply riding a trolley car in New Orleans and proclaiming Johnson's victory when a white man fatally stabbed him.

The rioting and racism of 1910 surrounding Johnson's victory were symptoms of the larger race problem that would continue in the nation throughout the twentieth century. However, Johnson's victory did help to carve the way for future black athletes to gain success, receiving fame and fortune instead of hatred and outrage.

Suggested Activities

Black Athletes: Learn about the accomplishments of other black athletes in the first portion of the twentieth century and how they broke ground for black athletes to come.

Boxing: Learn about the sport of boxing, how it is played, and who the significant boxers of history have been.

Discussion: Boxing has become a controversial sport. Some think it is a true test of physical skill while others say it is ruthlessly brutal and that it should be outlawed. Have the class discuss the issue.

The Great Migration

One of the biggest population shifts in the history of the United States occurred during the period around World War I as thousands of African Americans left their homes and farms in the South and migrated north to industrial cities in search of employment. The results of this shift were far-reaching, changing the course of African-American history.

When the migrating black population came to urban areas and began to work *en masse* in industries — particularly those industries vacated by white men who had gone overseas to fight the war—the expansion of the black base in urban communities resulted in greater business opportunities for blacks. Consequently, racial pride grew even in the face of rampant racism. Meanwhile, the numbers of educated blacks (individuals who were educated academically rather than vocationally) grew, and these people often became strong sociopolitical leaders for the entire community. Many of these leaders encouraged the use of wartime to make advances for the race as a whole. Employment and educational opportunities seemed just the way to do that.

Of course, many blacks also served in the war. There were approximately 370,000 servicemen in all, and while the majority of those individuals served on support units, many were a part of all-black regiments with extensive combat experiences. In fact, the first Allied regiment to reach the Rhine River was the 369th Infantry, a black regiment. Black soldiers returning from the war came home with an even more impassioned demand for the respect for which they had fought and so richly deserved.

The times were changing rapidly for African Americans of the decade. Indeed, the mass migration, increased education, and greater job opportunities became much of the basis for the creative and intellectual renaissance that was to sweep the black community in the next decade. Newspapers and magazines published by blacks were distributed in many areas, and renowned black musicians and authors were coming to the forefront of the nation's artistic community. Blacks began to gather in social and political organizations with a new sense of purpose which laid the foundation for the awakening that was to come.

Suggested Activities

Chronicler: The artist Jacob Lawrence was born in 1917, and he grew up to chronicle the lives of his and other families that were part of the Great Migration of the time. His migration series consisted of a set of sixty numbered panels that told the story of the people who made the choice to move away from their homes. Research Lawrence and his paneled series.

Response: Ask students to respond to the question, "What sacrifices did people make in migrating north?" If students have a hard time answering this, start by asking them what sacrifices they would have to make if they were to move to a different geographical location.

Creative Writing: Direct students to write a creative story about the family members who were left behind.

UNIA: Research the life of Marcus Garvey and the Universal Negro Improvement Association, established in 1916. It was very much a part of the changing way of life for African Americans of the time.

The Unsinkable *Titanic*

In April of 1912, approximately 2,200 passengers and crew members boarded the *Titanic*, a new luxury liner ready for its maiden voyage. The *Titanic* had the best of everything, and only the elite could afford passage. Some paid more than $4,000 for the trip, while many of the crew did not even earn $1,000 in a year. The ship's promoters claimed that their vessel was unsinkable, primarily because its hull had sixteen watertight compartments. Even if two compartments flooded, the ship would still float. Everyone had complete confidence in the boat.

A number of famous people were on board, including millionaire John Jacob Astor and his wife, as well as Isidor and Ida Straus, the wealthy department-store owners. In general, the passengers had complete confidence in the ship because the best design and latest technology were at their service.

Late on the night of April 14, the *Titanic* was sailing in the North Atlantic Ocean on its trip from Southampton, England, to New York City. The ship was traveling at a speed of twenty-one knots (nautical miles per hour), which was nearly its top speed. Since there was danger of icebergs in the area, the ship's speed was far too fast. At 11:40 P.M., the *Titanic* scraped alongside an iceberg for approximately ten seconds. That was enough. The hull of the ship was made of a type of steel that became brittle in icy waters such as those of the North Atlantic. Several small cracks appeared instantly, and seams unriveted. Water started to pour inside, weakening the hull still further.

Six distress signals were sent out immediately. Another passenger ship, the *California*, was just twenty minutes away at the time; however, its radio operator was not on duty, so no one there heard the *Titanic's* signal. Another ship, the *Carpathia*, was approximately four hours away, and it responded to the signal. However, when the *Carpathia* arrived at 4:00 A.M., it was too late for many of the passengers. The *Titanic* had long since sunk. Just after 2:00 A.M., water had flooded through the hull to the ship's bow, causing the entire vessel to split in two.

At first, the passengers aboard the ship were calm, expecting to reach lifeboats with ease and then be rescued by other ships. They did not know that the *Titanic's* lifeboats only had spaces for approximately 1,200 people, far fewer than the number of people on board. When the passengers and crew saw how dire the situation was, many stepped aside for younger passengers to board lifeboats safely. Among these heroes were the Astors and Strauses. Captain Edward J. Smith went down with his ship. In all, 705 people survived the wreck, most of them women and children. The remaining 1,517 died in the icy waters of the North Atlantic Ocean.

When the ship was first endangered, the band on board began to play a ragtime melody to encourage the passengers. As time passed and the situation grew grim, they continued to play; at that point, however, their musical selections included an old English hymn calling for mercy and compassion from God.

In 1985, a team of scientists found the wreckage of the *Titanic* 12,500 feet (3,800 meters) beneath the sea. Although people had previously thought that a large gash was immediately ripped in the boat because of the iceberg, the scientists were able to prove that the steel composition of the hull was truly the fatal flaw, and that flaw, combined with the speed at which the boat was traveling, led to its demise.

Suggested Activities

Read: Find reports of the studies made from the 1985 expedition. What did they reveal about the ship and its passengers? What did the scientists do to find the wreck?

Writing: Imagine you are a *Titanic* survivor, floating away on a lifeboat while hundreds of others are struggling in the freezing water. Write what you think and experience.

38

The Grand Canyon: "Beautiful, Terrible, and Unearthly"

Located in northern Arizona, the breathtaking Grand Canyon National Park was established in 1919. The park encompasses the Colorado River's course from Glen Canyon National Recreation Area to the Lake Mead National Recreation Area—and, of course, all of the canyon itself.

Surprisingly, early explorers of the canyon were generally not impressed. Army Lieutenant Joseph Ives wrote in 1857, "The region is of course altogether valueless." Major John Wesley Powell wrote in 1869 that the canyon, which towered above him and his men while they sailed down the Colorado, was a "granite prison." Many of these unimpressed individuals happened upon the canyon at its southern rim, which tourists from around the world know to be less awe-inspiring than the northern area; even so, the entire Canyon is an amazing example of the power of nature and the history of the earth's development. As President Theodore Roosevelt said in 1903, "It is beautiful, terrible, and unearthly. Leave it as it is. You cannot improve on it."

The Grand Canyon has been inhabited for perhaps as long as five thousand years by Native American populations. The Anasazi and Cohonina lived within and farmed the canyon by 1100 A.D., and in 1150 A.D., the Cerbats came to the area. The Cerbats are the direct ancestors of the Havasupai and Hualapai, groups which are among those who live in the canyon today.

For many years, when Americans were developing the rest of the country, they left the canyon alone to the native people who called it home. This is probably due to the fact that exploration and inhabitation of the canyon were difficult. However, by the late nineteenth century, a national interest was awakened, and in 1901 the Santa Fe Railroad laid a track directly to the canyon. Tourist accommodations quickly began to arise.

There were attempts at legislation to protect the area as a national park as early as 1886. In 1906, President Roosevelt enacted legislation to create the Grand Canyon Game Preserve, followed by the declaration of the area as a national monument in 1908. When statehood came to Arizona, the state's citizens joined in an effort to have the canyon named a national park. President Woodrow Wilson signed the Grand Canyon National Park Act on February 26, 1919, making the canyon the seventeenth national park within the United States.

The popularity of the Grand Canyon has risen rapidly and steadily over the years. In 1919, the park saw approximately 44,000 visitors, more than one million annually by the mid-fifties, and five million annually today. People come to see its beauty and majesty and to be awed by the variety and scope of its geology.

Suggested Activities

Geology: Learn about the geological history and formation of the Canyon. Break into small groups to study the different areas. Share group findings as a class.

Math: Research to find the Canyon's dimensions, then work mathematical equations, using those figures, to determine areas, proportions, ratios, and so forth.

Like Father, Like Son

By 1910, American cities were growing astronomically. There were myriad new buildings intended to "scrape the sky" and mechanized technology that could transport, protect, and arm. Is it any wonder that while the adult world built upwards and outwards, the world's children began to do the same?

Prior to this time, children had mimicked adult constructions with whatever materials they had available, from the sticks and stones they found outdoors to the building blocks that could be purchased at the local mercantile shop. However, when structural steel was developed and went into regular use in buildings and machinery, some forward-thinking individuals took the idea a step further to prepare a new type of "building blocks" for children, who could then create small-scale structures like the new ones being built around them.

Many manufacturers of such products came rapidly into being, but three products quickly came to the forefront: Erector® Sets, Tinker Toys®, and Lincoln Logs®.

Erector® Sets: Created out of the desire for educational toys, Erector® Sets were first sold in 1913 at the New York City Toy Show. They were the creation of Alfred Carlton Gilbert, a former Olympic gold medalist and a doctor, who also dabbled in magic. While on a train trip to New York, Gilbert saw steel poles being erected to carry electric lines for trains. He began to think that children might enjoy partaking in such constructive efforts as well, but on their own scale. Gilbert worked through several prototypes to perfect his idea. The first Erector® Set consisted of metal strips, as well as the nuts, bolts, pinions, and gears that were necessary to attach them and allow them to move. The sets came in large wooden boxes, and the largest sets included electric motors that children could also assemble. Strange by modern standards, the manuals that came with the kits included illustrated pictures of finished projects but no written directions for how to create them. The idea was that everything should come from the child's imagination. One year after its first sale, 60,000 submissions were entered into the company's first model-building contest for children. By the time its creator retired in 1956, more than 40 million Erector® Sets had been sold.

Tinker Toys®: While older children used their Erector® Sets, younger children could build with Tinker Toys®. Tinker Toys® are colorful wooden dowels, discs, and spools which can be connected by placing the dowels through holes in the other pieces. They were created by Charles Pajeau in 1914. He got the idea while watching children play with sticks and spools of thread, inserting the sticks through the spools to connect the pieces.

Lincoln Logs®: In 1866 a toy called Log Cabin Playhouses came into being; but the Lincoln Logs we know today were designed by John Lloyd Wright, the son of the world-renowned architect Frank Lloyd Wright, in 1915. John Lloyd Wright got the idea for his toy directly from one of his father's works: the cantilever (supported on one end) design the elder Wright used in constructing the Imperial Hilton of Tokyo. Today, more than ten million sets of Lincoln Logs® have been sold.

Suggested Activity

Compare: The biggest-selling construction toys today are LEGO® and K'Nex®; however, all of the toys listed above can still be found on the market. As a class, experiment with each of the toys and make comparison graphs as to their versatility and usability.

Nine-Letter Word for Fun

Open any number of magazines today, and you are sure to find one. They are so commonplace it is difficult to imagine that someone actually invented them! But someone did, and it is because of Arthur Wynne in 1913 that we have crossword puzzles today.

Arthur Wynne was an editor for *New York World* magazine in 1913 when he found himself short on copy for the "Fun" section in the December 21 edition. Struggling to come up with a filler for the space, Wynne recalled the word game his grandfather had introduced to him. The game was called Word Square, and in it, the individual would attempt to arrange a list of words in a square so that they would be read the same across and down. Wynne liked the idea, but he thought he could improve upon it. Using different words for the horizontal and vertical lines, Wynne provided only the grid which his readers would have to fill in based on the clues he gave. He called his puzzle Word-Cross. The puzzle was a huge success, and the readers quickly begged for a new puzzle each week. When a typesetter carelessly switched the words of the puzzle's name, it became known as Cross-Word. The rest is "a seven-letter word for 'past events.'" (*History*!)

Suggested Activity

Do It Yourself: Make your own crossword puzzle, using the grid below. Follow the guidelines laid out by Wynne's successor, Margaret Petherbridge Farrar, whose crossword career spanned sixty years: 1. Use a symmetrical grid. 2. Make the words interlock throughout the puzzle. 3. Use a minimal number of black spaces. 4. Do not use one- or two-letter words. Try it!

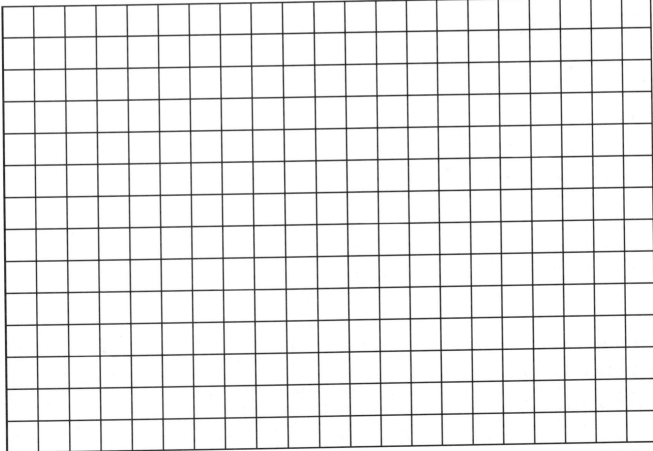

Hooray for Hollywood

Today, Hollywood is renowned as the moviemaking capital of the world, but that was not always the case. It had to begin somewhere—or with someone. That someone was Cecil B. De Mille.

The Nestor Company built the first film studio in Hollywood in 1911, but it was De Mille who brought the area notoriety and made it the film center of the United States. When sent to produce *The Squaw Man* in Flagstaff, Arizona, De Mille promptly turned away from the flatlands of Arizona and headed for sunny California. Hollywood was a prime location with its mild climate and close proximity to a variety of natural settings. It was small and quiet, a country town surrounded by lemon groves. De Mille rented a barn in Hollywood and began his project.

In and of themselves, the director's experiences while making the film could have made for interesting cinematic subject matter. Someone sabotaged his first negative, he was shot at twice, and he had to sleep in the barn—with the owner's horses—in order to protect himself and his remaining negative. De Mille also went overboard on his budget, tripling the scheduled cost. When the film was finally shown, it was wrongly perforated and needed to be redone. However, after all the trouble and turmoil of creating that one, simple movie, De Mille found himself with a hit on his hands.

Other producers and directors flocked to Hollywood to take advantage of the location. So many came, in fact, that by 1914, some boarding houses had hung signs that read: "No dogs, no actors." Nonetheless, the number of movie people coming to Hollywood grew so rapidly that soon it became the movie capital that we know today.

A small group of actors and a director were also influential in beginning Hollywood's movie fame. They called themselves the United Artists. The United Artists was a movie-making organization begun in 1919 by actors Charlie Chaplin, Douglas Fairbanks, Sr., and Mary Pickford, and director D. W. Griffith. They started the company in order to have greater creative control in the movies they made. Chaplin was known as the Little Tramp, and he was a Hollywood favorite by this time. Fairbanks made his film debut in 1915, but became a Hollywood staple in the 1920s. Mary Pickford and Fairbanks married in 1920, when she was already a star known as "America's Sweetheart" (page 63). Griffith was highly influential in turning filmmaking into an art form. The film production strategies he developed from 1908 to 1912 became the basis for moviemaking. From 1913 on, he was an influential Hollywood director.

By 1916, 52 companies were headquartered in Hollywood. In just six years, the once little country town became the movie mecca of the world.

Suggested Activities

Movies: Trace the history of movies. Have the students report on famous movie stars, influential business leaders, moviemaking awards, and the technical aspects of film production.

People: Learn more about the lives of De Mille, Chaplin, Fairbanks, Pickford, and Griffith.

Industry: The city of Hollywood—which is actually a district of Los Angeles—became the center of the moviemaking industry. Have the class brainstorm and research to find other towns that are central to other industries.

Daylight Saving Time

"Spring forward, fall back." Every schoolchild learns the phrase. But does every child know why we do it? The "it," of course, is Daylight Saving Time. The "why" dates back to World War I.

Britain introduced Daylight Saving Time, or "Summertime" as they called it, in 1916. America followed in 1918, and in both cases, World War I was the reason.

Both nations got the idea from a humorous essay published by Benjamin Franklin in 1784. Franklin's idea was presented more seriously in 1907 by a British builder named William Willett in his pamphlet, *Waste of Daylight.*

When war broke out, Britain looked for a way to conserve precious fuel that was necessary to produce electricity. "Extending" daylight another hour into the evening seemed a sensible choice. When the United States joined the war, the nation decided to follow suit. Many other nations used this light-saving device throughout the war years as well. After the war, some countries reverted to the old system of time while others maintained daylight saving.

Daylight Saving Time is simply brought about. Clocks are set ahead by one or two hours so that sunrise and sunset both occur later, resulting in an additional hour of light in the evening. In the Western world, clocks are set ahead by one or two hours in the spring and set back again in the fall.

When World War II erupted, the United States used Daylight Saving Time once again, this time calling it "Wartime." Wartime was maintained throughout the entire length of the war. Britain followed suit, and during the summer months, Britain moved its clocks forward another hour still.

Due to controversy regarding the Daylight Saving program, the United States developed the Uniform Time Act in 1966, a system of uniform time within individual time zones. States may exempt themselves, however, when their own legislature votes to keep standard time. Otherwise, every state moves its clocks forward one hour at 2 A.M. on the first Sunday of April and back one hour at 2 A.M. on the last Sunday of October, as per legislation enacted in 1986.

Controversy surrounding the program continues even today, with many people wondering at the necessity of changing time when no conservation is required. Individuals within certain businesses have particular complaints, such as farmers whose work is done according to the sun and who have difficulties altering their business schedules because of time changes, or airlines and railroads which may have difficulties dealing with interstate traveling when all areas concerned are not participants in the Daylight Saving program. However, many other people enjoy the time change, particularly the additional evening hour of daylight during the summer holidays. Undoubtedly, the debate will continue as time invariably marches on.

Suggested Activities

Science: Learn about the nature of time and how the modern understanding of time has developed through the years. Perhaps you might also consider the possibility of time travel and the meaning of relativity.

Math: Solve a variety of equations that deal with time, particularly time from one area to another, and especially those areas (such as the state of Arizona) which do not use Daylight Saving Time.

Debate: Should Daylight Saving Time be used today? Poll the class to see what the consensus is. Then divide the class into two groups and research the issue. Hold a debate, arguing both sides of the case. Then, poll the class once more to see if any opinions have changed. If so, discuss why; and if not, discuss why not.

The Black Sox

It was a dark time for baseball in 1919. The greatest team in the nation, the Chicago White Sox, was involved in a scandal from which it would take the team decades to recover.

The White Sox team of 1919 was one of the best ever. Eddie Cicotte and Claude "Lefty" Williams were extraordinary pitchers who threw like lightning. Joseph Jefferson Jackson, nicknamed "Shoeless Joe" because he once played without shoes rather than wear a new pair which had given him blisters, had a lifetime batting average of .356, still the third-highest in baseball history. The team easily took the American League pennant, and they were shoo-ins to win the World Series. Instead, they lost, and one year later, eight players on the team were permanently barred from baseball. Here is what happened.

The White Sox and the Cincinnati Reds faced off in game one of the Series. Just as play began, rumors started to spread that the White Sox were planning to *throw* the Series, meaning they were intentionally going to lose in exchange for money. Cicotte did, in fact, lose the opening game by a score of 9-1, and Williams lost the second, 4-2. By this point, many felt the rumors of illegal activities to be true. While the White Sox would win three of the next five games, their play was inconsistent and at times baffling: Cicotte and others made crucial fielding errors that were completely uncharacteristic of their usual style of play, Williams pitched horribly, and the White Sox batters were unable to produce, especially in clutch situations. "Shoeless" Joe Jackson, however, did bat .375—an exceptional mark by any standards—and hit the Series' only home run. In the eighth game, the White Sox were beaten soundly, 10-5. The Series was over; the fans were stunned. How could a team as dominating as the White Sox be so unimpressive in defeat?

For the next several months, there were many rumors that the players on the team had accepted bribes from gamblers in exchange for losing the Series. If the gamblers could be certain of the White Sox's loss, they could clean up by betting for the underdogs, the Cincinnati Reds.

One year later, eight team members were arrested: Cicotte, Williams, Jackson, Chick Gandil, Happy Felsch, Swede Risberg, Fred McMullin, and Buck Weaver. According to the indictment, first baseman Chick Gandil took money from gamblers and passed it among the other players on the team. Reporters started referring to the team as the Black Sox. Fans were heartbroken, and they did not want to believe it was true. A story was circulated at the time that as Joe Jackson left the Chicago Courthouse, he was stopped by a young boy who tugged on the ballplayer's sleeve, looked up with tears in his eyes, and said, "Say it ain't so, Joe."

Although a jury in the civil trial aquitted the eight players, baseball commissioner Kenesaw Mountain Landis permanently barred them from professional baseball. The White Sox would not win another pennant for forty years, and they have yet to win a post-scandal World Series. Perhaps it is taking this long to live down the legacy of the Black Sox scandal.

Suggested Activities

Skits: In small groups, have the students write skits enacting different scenes from the White Sox scandal. They can perform their skits for one another.

Play Ball: During physical education time, learn the basics of baseball and play a game.

Debate: When Shoeless Joe died in 1951, among his dying words were "I don't deserve this thing that's happened to me. I'm going to meet the greatest umpire of all—and He knows I'm innocent." Jackson never asked to be reinstated in baseball. There are those who believe that because of his lifetime batting record, he should be enshrined in Baseball's Hall of Fame. Form sides to debate the question. Research to learn what needs to be done to clear the name of Shoeless Joe.

The Georgia Peach

Tyrus Raymond Cobb was born in Banks County, Georgia, in 1886. Little did his proud parents know that their baby boy would become a baseball legend known as "The Georgia Peach."

Ty Cobb spent an amazing twenty-four years as a professional baseball player. He was with the Detroit Tigers from 1905 until 1926, and he was their manager from 1921 until he left the team. In 1927 and 1928, he played with the Philadelphia Athletics.

During his long career, Cobb made and held a number of baseball records. He is the all-time leading hitter in the major leagues, with a lifetime batting average of .367. His career total of 4,191 hits was not surpassed until Pete Rose did so in 1985. Cobb won twelve American League batting titles, nine of them in a row from 1907 to 1915. He was certainly a crucial part of his team's three pennants in a row from 1907 to 1909.

Ty Cobb

Besides his excellent batting, Cobb was known for his baserunning ability. During his long career, he stole 892 bases, and in 1915, he established the record (since broken) for most bases stolen in a season (96). Also, he had a reputation as a fierce player who used rough play to intimidate the other team. This aggressive playing nature, coupled with his quickness, enabled him to be a stolen-base leader. Cobb frequently turned a base hit into a double or triple by stealing bases. Once, he gained two bases on a bunt.

Cobb used whatever legal methods he could to intimidate his rivals, but it was also rumored that he sharpened the spikes of his cleats. If true, this would certainly have gotten the attention of the opposing teams.

Of course, although Cobb's stealing of bases might be chalked up to aggression, his outstanding hitting was pure talent. In his first year, he hit only .240, but in each year after that he hit no less than .300. (In major league baseball, hitting .300 is generally considered the benchmark for batting excellence.)

As a final triumph, Ty Cobb was one of the first five players elected to the newly established National Baseball Hall of Fame in 1936. This is a feat that can never be surpassed.

Suggested Activities

Stealing Bases: During physical education time, practice stealing bases. See who can rival Ty Cobb—not for his rough playing but for his success.

Classroom Baseball: Hold a mock baseball game in class. Prepare a number of questions or problems in the subject areas you are studying. Divide the class into two teams, and designate them as "home" and "visitors" or allow them to select team names. Draw a scoreboard on the chalkboard. The "pitcher" reads a question for a "batter" of the opposing team. Score a base hit for a correctly answered question or a strike for a wrong answer. You may choose to adjust the scoring so that an answer with several parts is a double or triple or a single incorrect answer is a strikeout. Recycle any questions that receive incorrect answers. Three outs and the other team is up to bat. Play nine innings in all, if you like.

Jim Thorpe

Jim Thorpe is widely considered one of the greatest athletes of all time. His talents ranged from football to baseball to track and field, and he was successful at the highest level in all of those sports. Born in Oklahoma in 1887, Thorpe, a Native American, began to show his athletic skill at the Carlisle Indian Industrial School in Pennsylvania. Because of him, the small school achieved national recognition.

Jim Thorpe

In the 1912 Olympics in Stockholm, Sweden, Thorpe became the first athlete to win both the pentathlon and decathlon. He also came in first in the 200-meter dash and the 1,500-meter run. Russia's Tsar Nicholas II sent Thorpe a silver model of a Viking ship as a tribute to his skill, and the King of Sweden called him "the greatest athlete in the world." Thorpe had earned a small salary as a baseball player in 1909 and 1910, and because this gave him professional status and not the amateur status required to compete in Olympic games, his medals were taken away about a month after he received them. In 1982, twenty-nine years after Thorpe's death, the International Olympic Committee reconsidered and restored the medals.

A multitalented athlete, Jim Thorpe played professional baseball for three major league teams (1913–1919) and football for seven teams (1915–1930). He became the first president of the American Professional Football Association (now the National Football League) and one of the first men admitted into the National Football Foundation's Hall of Fame (1951). Today, though athletes show masterful skills in their respective fields, it is quite rare for a single athlete to compete successfully in even two different sports.

Suggested Activities

Pentathlon: As a tribute to Thorpe, and as a means to show your own athletic skill, hold your own classroom pentathlon. The traditional events are the long jump, javelin throw, 200-meter run, discus throw, and 1,500-meter run. These, however, are not conducive to the classroom. Choose five activities that will comprise your pentathlon. They can be fun, like banana tossing or hopscotch. Most importantly, have fun!

Olympics: The Olympic Games of 1912 were also notable for two other reasons. They were the first Olympics that allowed women to compete, although they only did so in swimming and diving. Find out more about these groundbreaking women athletes of the 1912 games. The second reason is that the Americans won thirteen out of the twenty-eight possible golds. Who were the gold medal winners of the 1912 Olympics?

Multitalented Athletes: Some athletes have played professionally in more than one sport, including Bo Jackson and Deion Sanders. Name any other athletes you can who have done this and tell the sports in which they have played. Have any of them been as successful in two or more sports as Jim Thorpe was?

Knute Rockne

Knute Kenneth Rockne is considered today to be one of the greatest college football players and coaches of all time. Born in Voss, Norway, in 1888, Rockne and his family moved to Chicago, Illinois, in 1893. Raised in American schools, Rockne received his college education at Notre Dame University, outside of South Bend, Indiana. While at Notre Dame, Rockne became one of the football team's leading players.

Football at that time, although popular, was still developing into the game we know today. Absent was the extensive protective gear modern players wear. Padding was minimal, and helmets were merely leather caps strapped under the chin. The game was physical, and the dangers of playing it were, in many ways, even higher than they are today.

The game of the day was almost exclusively a running one, with the ball being pitched and run down the field for the score. In 1906, a new offensive technique was introduced. It was called the forward pass. Although little used, Rockne employed it while he was captain of the Notre Dame football team in 1912. It became his signature offensive ploy. The move quickly caught the nation's attention, and while Rockne's popularity grew, so did the use of the forward pass. When Notre Dame, under the leadership of Rockne, beat the highly favored Army team—by far the superior team in strength and size—by a score of 35–13, much of their success was due to Rockne and the forward pass. Rockne's instant popularity benefited the sport as a whole in that it extended football's fan base dramatically.

In 1914, Rockne became assistant football coach for Notre Dame, and in 1918, he took over as head coach. He kept that position until 1931 when he died tragically in an airplane crash. During Rockne's career as coach, he led Notre Dame to three championships, 105 wins, twelve losses, five ties, and a total of 2,847 points scored.

Today when people think of Notre Dame and college football, they often think of Knute Rockne. His legacy is an important part of the game's history.

Suggested Activities

Physical Education: As a class, play a game of touch football.

Compare and Contrast: Learn about the game of football in 1912 and compare it to college football today. Also, compare American football to European football—what Americans call soccer. Finally, compare college football with professional football. How are each of these the same, and how are they different?

Debate: Football is a highly physical sport, and injuries are commonplace. Debate the pros and cons of playing football. Is it too dangerous to be played?

Tournament of Roses: The 1910s also saw the beginning of the Rose Bowl game. (While the first Rose Bowl was played in 1906, yearly Bowls did not begin until 1916.) Study the history of the Rose Bowl and how a team is chosen to play.

Jim Thorpe: Another great football player of the day was Jim Thorpe. Learn about his life and experiences. (See page 46.)

Tanks

Existing wheeled armored vehicles used to transport artillery did not maneuver well in mud or over trenches. As a result, the British developed the *tank*, a kind of armored landship that moves on a caterpillar tread system, enabling it to cover almost any terrain. Because the new vehicles were shipped in crates marked "water tank" to conceal their purpose from the enemy, they became known simply as tanks. The first tanks were used against the Germans in the Battle of the Somme in 1916. During this battle, they were slow and difficult to operate. An eight-man crew was required for the first tanks, including four men to steer. Improvements followed quickly, and tanks were used successfully in the Battle of Cambrai in 1917. By the end of the war, Britain had built 2,350 tanks of 13 different types. France built some 4,000 lightweight tanks. The war ended before America could manufacture any.

Tanks have continued to play major roles in wars since then. In World War II, every fighting nation used tanks. The German armored divisions, called *panzers*, were especially successful during the war. In 1944, tanks helped the Allies sweep across Germany, paving the way for victory in the war.

As tanks became an important part of the arsenal, weapons were developed specifically to stop them. In the Arab-Israeli War of 1973, over 6,000 tanks were used, but almost half of them were destroyed just 18 days into the war by precision-guided missiles that easily wiped them out. In the Persian Gulf War of 1991, the United States used more than 2,000 tanks, and few were lost. However, Iraq lost in excess of 3,500 tanks. This statistic showed that tanks were still useful, but weaponry and experience were even more important.

Below is a model of a U.S. Army M1A1 battle tank. The tank is covered in armor, and particularly heavy armor covers the front end behind which the driver sits. The engine and transmission are in the back, and a continuous track rolls underneath. The gunner sits behind the driver, and the commander sits behind him or her, also acting as a gunner. The loader sits behind the commander but in front of the ammunition. Above the crew is the machine gun, and to the front of the tank is the 120-mm gun.

Suggested Activity

Components: Label the elements of the tank diagram. Use the word bank below.

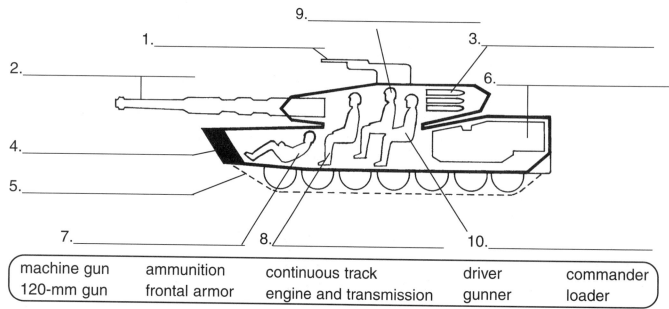

| machine gun | ammunition | continuous track | driver | commander |
| 120-mm gun | frontal armor | engine and transmission | gunner | loader |

Submarines

Submarines are ships that travel under the water. Most are designed for use during war. They are made of material that is able to endure the pressure of the sea. A submarine generally has a propeller, rudders, and diving planes in the back and a periscope, diving planes, a hatch, and a radar system above. It also has tubes for shooting torpedoes.

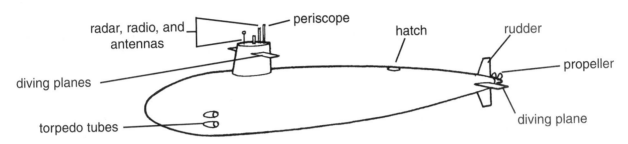

Submarines were used successfully as warships for the first time during World War I. Here is a history of their development prior to the Great War and their usage during it.

1620 The first useable submarine was invented by Cornelius van Drebbel, a Dutch scientist. It was a wooden rowboat covered with waterproof hides.

1776 The *Turtle* was used in the Revolutionary War. It was a one-man submarine, created by Yale student David Bushnell. It was operated by a hand-cranked propeller. It attempted to sink a British warship in New York Harbor but failed. However, this was the first time a submarine was used to attack another boat.

1800 The *Nautilus* was invented by Robert Fulton, an American. During demonstrations, it sank a number of ships. However, neither Britain nor France, to whom Fulton tried to sell his copper-covered vessel, was interested in purchasing it.

1864 The *Hunley*, a Confederate submarine, became the first underwater ship to sink another ship in wartime. It used an explosive attached to a long pole. It rammed the *Housatonic*, a Union ship, in Charleston Harbor; however, it sank with its target. The *Hunley* was found by a team of explorers in 1995.

1898 The U.S.S. *Holland* was sold to the United States Navy by American John P. Holland. It was the first U.S. submarine, and it was powered by gasoline engine and electric batteries.

1902 The periscope was invented by Simon Lake, an American. It used magnifying lenses so the submarine operators could see targets at a distance. Lake also invented wheels on submarines so they could drive along the ocean floor.

1908 The first diesel-powered submarines were used by the British. Most submarines were diesel-powered until the 1950s, when nuclear power was developed.

1914–1918 Germany used the submarine as a lethal warship. A German submarine was known as a U-boat, short for *Unterseeboot*. U-boats sank many enemy ships, including merchant and passenger vessels. The sinking of U.S. ships by Germany's submarines was influential in the U.S.'s eventual entry into the war.

The most infamous attack by a U-boat during World War I was the torpedoing of the *Lusitania* in 1915. Approximately 1,200 passengers were killed, including 128 Americans. (See page 16)

Suggested Activity

Types: Submarines come in two main types: attack and ballistic. Find out about the differences between the two, how they are powered, and how the crews live on them.

Carl Jung

Teacher Note: The content of Jung's theories could be sensitive subject matter. Discussion of it will require discretion.

Carl Jung

Carl Gustav Jung was born in Basel, Switzerland, to a minister. When he was young, he was very interested in superstition and mythology. Jung entered the University of Basel in 1895 and studied archeology; however, his interests changed. In 1902, he graduated from the University of Zurich as a physician. He then began a psychiatric practice in Zurich.

At first, Jung followed the practices of Sigmund Freud, and in 1907, the two became close friends. However, they split in 1913, partly because Jung believed that Freud emphasized the importance of sexual instincts too strongly, but also because Jung saw broader applications for the field of psychology than did Freud. From that time forward, Jung developed his own theories of the unconscious and human relationships. He also spent a long period of time analyzing himself.

In 1917, Jung published his great work, *Psychology of the Unconscious*. In it, the reader can learn much of what Jung theorized. Like Freud, Jung believed that everyone is driven by his or her unconscious mind, the place where personal drives and desires reside. However, Jung did not believe that sexuality was really important to a person until puberty. Jung asserted that the personalities of a child's parents have great influence on that child. He also believed that people share a *collective unconscious* through which they are all connected regardless of race, time, and experience. In the collective unconscious there are archetypes, thought patterns that everyone has over different ways of being. These archetypes allow people to think and react just as their ancestors did. Jung felt that great wisdom could be found in the collective unconscious and that therapy could be used to help people uncover it.

Perhaps most significantly, Jung developed the concepts of *introvert* and *extrovert*. He said that an introvert is a person who depends primarily on himself or herself to get his or her needs met. An extrovert relies on the company of others for fulfillment of needs. Jung felt therapy could be useful to people in helping them balance themselves as both introverts and extroverts.

Throughout his career, Jung went back to the concepts in superstition and mythology that he enjoyed so much when he was a child. He believed that they were linked to the archetypes that existed in the collective unconscious. Religion, in particular, helped people express their unconscious need for this collective fulfillment.

Suggested Activities

Venn Diagram: Study both Jung and Freud, two important theorists of the early twentieth century, using a Venn diagram. Discuss what you find.

Introvert and Extrovert: Devise a test to determine if a person is a stronger introvert or extrovert. This test should be a series of questions that provide people with two choices for answers. For example, at a party, do you usually talk a lot with one or two people or visit briefly with many people? An introvert would tend to do the former and an extrovert the latter.

Vitamins

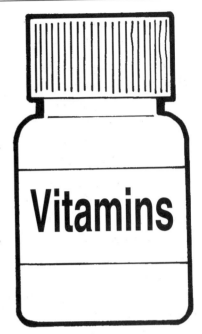

Vitamins are essential parts of the diet of living things; however, it was not until 1912 that vitamins were actually identified as such. Here is their history.

While carbohydrates, fat, and protein make up 98% of the dry weight consumed by people, the other 2% comes in vitamins and nutrients. The importance of these nutrients was recognized for the first time in the Middle Ages. At that time, some fortressed cities were cut off from fresh supplies while they were under siege. The deterioration of health (and sometimes even death) resulted from this lack of fresh provisions. Then, in the early 1500s, when prolonged voyages became a possibility, deficiency diseases aboard ships were common. For example, during Queen Elizabeth's reign at the end of the 16th century, approximately 10,000 men in her navy died of scurvy. The men were amply provided for with approximately 4,000 calories a day, including hardbread biscuits, salted meat or dried fish, butter, cheese, dried peas, and beer—rations which contained everything that people thought was necessary for a healthful life. Instead, the men developed rotten gums, loose teeth, bad breath, swollen cheeks, bruises, and aches and pains—all the signs of scurvy. Physicians at the time determined that certain medicines made of plants cured the scurvy.

Elsewhere, the Japanese navy was experiencing something similar, this time with a disease called *beri-beri*. Sometimes as much as two-thirds of a Japanese crew became afflicted with the disease. Through these experiences, it was learned that fresh plants were vital to a healthy life.

In 1906, Sir Frederick Galen Hopkins wrote an article stating that "accessory nutrients" were needed to maintain good health. In 1912, a substance was isolated from rice polish. It was an accessory nutrient that could prevent beri-beri. Vital for the preservation of life, it was also an *amine* (amino acid-like substance). These two words were combined, and the nutrient was called a "vitamine."

Many experiments were conducted on animals, testing the power of vitamines—now vitamins. The first such experiment to isolate and name a particular vitamin was also in 1912. Hopkins found that rats died on a diet of sugar, starch, fat, protein, and inorganic salts, but when they were also given a teaspoon of milk each day, they began to thrive. He believed that an "accessory food factor" was in the milk. He and others began to search for this accessory. Within a year, a fat-soluble substance was extracted from egg yolks, butter, and fish livers, and when it was removed from the rats' diets, their eyes became diseased. In 1913, researchers separated a water solution from rice bran, and this solution cured beri-beri. The extract from egg yolks and other foods was called "fat-soluble A," and the water solution was called "water-soluble B." In 1919, the first became known as vitamin A. Later it was called *retinol* because it was shown to be important to eyes and the retina. Over time, other vitamins were isolated and named; it is known today that these vitamins are also essential to good health.

Suggested Activities

Chart: Make a chart of the major vitamins and some of their sources.

Agriculture: As a class, choose several common vitamins and then find plants that contain them. Plant those seeds and care for them as they grow. When the vegetables are ready, eat them.

Transcontinental Telephone

Born in 1847 in Edinburgh, Scotland, Alexander Graham Bell's first and foremost interest was in speech, communication, and deafness. Bell's grandfather was a pioneer in the area of speech therapy, an interest shared by his son Melville, who was to become Bell's father. Bell's mother was an accomplished pianist, an amazing feat considering that she herself was deaf. It is with good reason that Bell took a lifelong interest in speech and hearing.

As a young man, Bell taught at the Boston School for the Deaf. It is there that he met his wife, Mabel Hubbard, and the man who would become his assistant, Thomas Watson. Watson, like Bell, was fascinated with the dynamics of sound.

With a curious and sharp mind, Bell turned to the world of invention. He worked particularly on two instruments: the harmonic telegraph, which could transmit a number of telegraph signals at the same time, and another device that could graphically record sound waves. Eventually, Bell saw the possibilities for connecting the two instruments. His goal was to create a single tool that could "transmit speech telegraphically."

On March 7, 1876, Alexander Graham Bell received a patent for the telephone, and on March 10 he made the first phone call to his assistant, Watson. Shortly thereafter, the telephone was exhibited to an enthusiastic public.

By 1900, more than one million telephones were in use in America, and by the early 1910s that number had multiplied by ten. However, the telephones of the time did not have the same capabilities enjoyed today. Telephone use was relatively local. Although Bell had conceived of a telephone system with wires laid underground or strung overhead, connecting through a main office, and allowing any two telephone sets to be in direct communication with one another, that reality had yet to happen.

However, thirty-nine years after their first phone call, Bell and Watson again achieved the impossible, moving a giant step closer to the telephone system first conceived by Bell. Calling from New York City, Bell reached Watson in San Francisco, thereby placing the first transcontinental phone call ever. The year was 1915, and the last telephone pole connecting the continent had just been set. "Mr. Watson," Bell said, "Come here, I want you." Watson answered, "Sorry, Mr. Bell, I can't. I'm too far away."

Since that time, telephone capabilities have crossed the oceans (the first transatlantic call was made in 1926), telephones have become cordless (1967), and most recently, cellular phones have come into common use (they were first used in 1983). Everywhere in the world, people can be connected with the push of a few buttons. It is amazing to think that it all began such a short while ago.

Suggested Activities

Technology: Learn about the technology of the telephone and how it has developed over time. How is today's technology like or different from that of Bell's time?

Monopoly: Many changes have happened in the telephone system in recent years. Once governed completely through a single company, telephone companies and services are now diverse and competitive. Trace this history and the reasons for the change.

Science: Many children have played the game of telephone whereby two cans are connected with a long string and used as a makeshift telephone. In small groups, invent your own "telephones," using everyday materials. Experiment with different types of string, rubber bands, wire, and so forth, comparing them to see which is the best carrier of sound.

The Pen Is Mightier Than the Sword

The 1910s were filled with quality literature by some of the world's finest writers. Here are three such writers who were popular at the time.

Jack London: John Griffith London was born in 1876 in San Francisco, California. He was raised in poverty by his mother, Flora Wellman, and her husband, John London. By the age of ten, the young boy was already working selling newspapers, and at fourteen he worked in a cannery. A series of other jobs followed in his teens, and by eighteen he was traveling the United States as a hobo. At about this time, he made a decision to live by his intellect and become a writer. London educated himself, reading and writing up to twenty hours per day. Just before the turn of the century, he sold his first story. By 1905, London had become the most widely read and highest paid author in America. Some of his novels include *The Call of the Wild*; *The Sea Wolf*; *White Fang*; and *John Barleycorn*, which is somewhat autobiographical.

London's books remained popular into the 1910s, although his publications in that decade did not match the success of the first. In 1916 at the age of forty, London died of a drug overdose.

Upton Sinclair: A muckraker* of the early twentieth century, Upton Beall Sinclair's work exposed social and political corruption. Many of his novels were based on actual events.

Born in 1878, Sinclair was a popular and influential author by 1906, when his best-known book, *The Jungle,* was published. Information in the book shocked President Roosevelt and influenced the passage of the Pure Food and Drug Act of the same year. From the 1910s forward, Sinclair became involved in politics and social causes. He was once a candidate for governor of California but was narrowly defeated. Also, he helped to form the American Civil Liberties Union and the League for Industrial Democracy. In 1943, he won the Pulitzer Prize for fiction. Sinclair died in 1968 after a long and successful career.

*A muckraker is a writer whose goal is to expose social and political problems and incite change.

Edith Wharton: Edith Wharton wrote of the middle class and aristocracy of New York society in the late nineteenth and early twentieth centuries. She herself was born into a prominent New York family in 1862, and she first achieved success in 1902 with *The Valley of Decision*. During World War I, her novels were greatly influenced by her experiences in wartime Paris. (She received the Cross of the Legion Honor for her relief work during the war.)

Wharton's books deal primarily with psychological characterizations of people faced with moral and social dilemmas. Some of her most famous works are *The Age of Innocence* (for which she won the Pulitzer Prize) and *Ethan Frome*. The works question the boundaries and mores of society; Wharton broke those boundaries in real life by supporting her husband throughout their marriage. When the two divorced in 1913, she moved to France. Wharton died in 1937 after many years of success.

Suggested Activities

Reading: Read excerpts from any of the above-named authors' works, carefully selecting passages appropriate for your class. London's *White Fang* and *The Call of the Wild* are probably the most accessible for young readers.

Writers: Each of these prominent writers of the 1910s exposed social, political, and/or cultural problems, although they did so in different ways. Write short stories with the same goals. Share them as a class and discuss the different ways in which students might meet the goals.

Zane Grey and the Story of the West

When critics think of the Western novel, the first name to come to mind is most likely to be Zane Grey. The author of more than fifty Westerns, several nonfiction books, and numerous articles on outdoor life, Grey himself lived through the final years of the Old West and into the dawn of the modern age.

Zane Grey was born in 1875 in Zanesville, Ohio. As a young man, Grey learned to be a dentist and began his adult life with that career. However, in 1904, he published his first novel, and the course of his life was changed. The novel was called *Betty Zane,* and it was based on the life of one of the author's ancestors.

Grey gave up dentistry for the life of an author. As the setting for most of his novels, he chose the Old West. He used it as the framework for such classic novels of the genre as *The Last of the Plainsmen* (1908), *The Thundering Herd* (1925), *Code of the West* (1934), and *West of the Pecos* (1937). One of his biggest selling novels ever was published in 1912. That novel, *Riders of the Purple Sage,* has become synonymous with the author.

Many of Grey's novels are popular even today. Some, including *Riders of the Purple Sage,* have been made into motion pictures. People today, just like those of the 1910s, are enthralled with the wild and exciting lives that were lived during the years of the untamed West. Grey had a knack for storytelling and a love of the time that draws the readers into his novels, making the West come alive again. Movies are a natural extension of Grey's writing.

Grey died in 1939. The days of the Old West were long gone by the time of his death, but they will always live on in the novels he left behind.

Suggested Activities

Historic Figures: Many real characters populate stories of the Old West, including Billy the Kid, Davy Crockett, General Custer, Crazy Horse, Sitting Bull, Chief Seattle, Annie Oakley, Buffalo Bill (page 66), and more. Research the lives of one of these figures. Tell the story of one interesting event in his or her life. If you can, write the story in the style of Zane Grey.

Compare: Zane Grey wrote about the Old West where life was often rough and wild. Elsewhere in the world at the same time, life could be much more civilized. Study a settled area in the eastern United States or elsewhere circa the same time period of Grey's novels. Then make a comparison of life at the same time in these two very different cultures.

Dime Novels: Dime novels came into being in the latter half of the 19th century. They were cheaply made paperback books that sold for ten cents apiece. They were highly melodramatic in tone, and their usual themes were crime, adventure, or history. The Western novel grew from the dime novel tradition. Learn more about dime novels and how Westerns got their start with them. Also learn how the dime novel business contributed to the change in publishing as a whole.

Read: Choose one of Grey's novels (Many are still in print.), read it, and report on it to the class. How would you describe Grey's style? Is the writing still interesting today?

Robert Frost

Robert Frost is among the most well-known and respected American poets of all time. Born in San Francisco, California, in 1874, Robert Lee Frost and his family moved to Lawrence, Massachusetts, in 1885, just after the death of his father. Frost completed high school in Lawrence, and then he attended college sporadically, spending time at Dartmouth and Harvard.

Never settling into a steady college routine, Frost left his studies and held a variety of odd jobs, which included working as a bobbin boy (in a wool mill), a shoemaker, a schoolteacher, and a newspaper editor. He became a farmer from 1900 to 1905, during which time he also turned to poetry. Discovering that writing poetry was his ultimate passion, Frost attempted to publish a collection of his works. With no success in his endeavors, Frost sold his farm in 1912 and left a teaching position in order to move to England. While there, he met a number of established poets, including Rupert Brooke and Edward Thomas. They were instrumental in helping Frost to reach his publishing goal.

A Boy's Will, Frost's first poetry collection, was published in England in 1913. In the following year, *North of Boston* was published, a collection which includes such classics as "Mending Wall" and "Home Burial." The two books were immediately successful, and Frost's reputation began to grow. Frost returned to the United States in 1915 and was able to publish his works there as well. From that point forward, his life as a poet was established.

Frost and his family moved to the New England area, owning farms in Vermont and New Hampshire. He continued to write poetry and began a collegiate profession as well, teaching literature at Amherst College, Harvard University, the University of Michigan, and Dartmouth.

Through the following years, Frost published many more volumes of poetry. *Mountain Interval* came in 1916, which included a poem that has become synonymous with Frost, "The Road Not Taken." *New Hampshire* arrived in 1923, and it was the first collection to show the touches of irony for which Frost is known. Perhaps the best remembered poem of that collection is "Stopping by the Woods on a Snowy Evening." Other volumes published during Frost's lifetime include *A Masque of Reason* (1945), *A Masque of Mercy* (1947), *West-Running Brook* (1928), *Witness Tree* (1942), *Steeple Bush* (1947), *Complete Poems* (1949), and *In the Clearing* (1962).

Through the years, Frost won four Pulitzer Prizes for his poetry, in 1924, 1931, 1937, and 1943. Although he always coveted the Nobel Prize, that particular award eluded him; however, he was honored by becoming the first poet to read his poetry at a presidential inauguration. In January 1961, Frost read "The Gift Outright" at John F. Kennedy's swearing-in ceremony.

Frost's poems are often philosophical. They sometimes take a moral bent, although irony and ambiguity are also common. The dialogue of the poems is usually colloquial while the verse and metrics remain traditional. (Frost abhorred free verse.) New England life was often Frost's subject, and he told of it in clear and simple language. In Frost's own words, poetry is "a momentary stay against confusion," and that is the essence of his work.

Suggested Activities

Biography: Frost's life is retold in three volumes, the first two written by Lawrence Thompson and published in 1966 and 1970, and the last written by R. H. Winnick, published in 1976. Read one or more to learn more about Frost's life.

Compare: Read some of Frost's poems, and then read some by Emily Dickinson and Ralph Waldo Emerson, two American poets to whom Frost's work is often compared. Make your own comparison. Consider style, language, and theme.

Modern Art and the Armory Show

In 1910, the world of art in America was classical and traditional. The rest of the world may have been changing, but the United States—culturally—kept to the status quo. What a surprise for the art world and the public when the Armory Show opened its doors.

Arthur B. Davies was a symbolist painter touring Europe when he saw the Soderbund Exhibit in Cologne in the summer of 1912. He immediately wired his friend Walt Kuhn about the extraordinary show, wondering why such a show featuring the work of contemporary artists could not happen in the United States. Kuhn decided to see it for himself, and he arrived on the last day of the exhibit. He was as enthralled as Davies. Cubism, Fauvism, and more were taking hold in the world of art. "Abstract" had become the new vogue, and the work was mesmerizing.

Kuhn decided that such a show could happen, and he was the man to do it. He set out to travel around Europe, meeting with artists and collectors, encouraging them to exhibit in the American show. The work was daunting, so he elicited the help of his friend Davies. With Davies' assistance, Kuhn was able to meet with numerous modern artists and collectors who agreed to take part in his ground-breaking endeavor.

Kuhn and Davies looked for a place in New York to showcase the collection. They had hopes of Madison Square Garden, but they thought the rental cost was too high. They decided upon the 69th Regiment Armory on Lexington Avenue between 25th and 26th. It was here on February 15, 1913, that the doors opened on the first American modern art exhibit, the Armory Show.

The show became one of the most talked- and written-about experiences of the time. Approximately 10,000 people paid admission daily during the show's one-month run. Attendees were split in their responses, although everyone's reaction was passionate. Viewers were either inspired or shocked, mesmerized or offended. New lines, new subjects, irony, ambiguity, irreverence—all were a part of this art that had never before been presented on American soil.

Eighteen rooms at the Armory held more than 13,000 works from such artists as Pablo Picasso, Paul Cézanne, Auguste Rodin, Constantin Brancusi, Marcel Duchamp, Georges Seurat, Henri Matisse, and Vincent van Gogh. Amazingly, such priceless works as Matisse's *Red Studio* and Cézanne's *Bathers* went unsold at the respective asking prices of $4,050 and $6,500.

People came to gaze and wonder at the works, but they also came to laugh and ridicule. Picasso's work was a common target of their jests, but perhaps most openly and frequently derided was Duchamp's *Nude Descending a Staircase*. Never before had a nude been shown in motion, and certainly never had such a figure been painted in such varying and geometric lines. People did not know what to make of it. Duchamp is said to have been amused by the fact that the work, which is now among the most valuable pieces of art in the world, sold for a mere $324.

When the show closed in New York, it went on to Chicago and Boston, creating the same fervor. In fact, art students in Chicago burned Matisse and Brancusi in effigy. However, by the time the show finally closed, more than 300,000 people had seen it. Little did they know they were witnessing history, for from that time forward, art in America made the leap from traditional to modern. In fact, many people say that modern art was born at the Armory Show.

━━━━━━━━━━━━━━ **Suggested Activity** ━━━━━━━━━━━━━━

Modern Art: View several pieces of art from this time period, particularly from the artists listed above. What is your response?

Duchamp

When one thinks of modern art, many names come to mind, such as Picasso, Matisse, and van Gogh. These artists were prolific, and certainly their work influenced the modern art movement. Yet there is one less prolific artist who certainly deserves to be named among his contemporaries, for his work was central to the change from traditional art to modern. His name is Marcel Duchamp.

Duchamp was born in Blainville, France, on July 28, 1887. His brother was the artist Raymond Duchamp-Villon, and his half-brother was the artist Jacques Villon. Duchamp himself began to paint in 1908.

Duchamp's earliest works are Fauvist. Fauvism was a movement in French painting from about 1898 to 1908. Color is key to Fauvist art. Prior to Fauvism, Impressionists used soft and shimmering colors, but Fauvists turned to impassioned and expressive colors in their works. They also utilized bold lines and dramatic patterns. The term Fauvism comes from *les fauves,* a French phrase meaning "the wild beasts." This was originally a negative name given to a group of artists in 1905. The name eventually became accepted in the mainstream as a label for the modern artists whose works conveyed such passion.

After his Fauvist period, Duchamp turned to avant-garde. It was then that he created *Nude Descending a Staircase,* the painting that would create such controversy and fervor at the Armory Show in February of 1913 (page 56). The painting showed continuous movement in a cubist style.

After 1915, Duchamp did not paint a great deal. However, he did work until 1923 on what many consider to be his masterpiece, *The Bride Stripped Bare by Her Bachelors, Even,* also known as *The Large Glass.* This abstract work is composed on glass using oil paint and wire. It was particularly well received by the surrealists, a group of artists who promoted the concept of the unconscious in all creative endeavors.

Duchamp began to create sculptures, and he is credited with two sculptural innovations: kinetic art and readymade art. The terms are fairly self-explanatory. Kinetic art depicts and expresses movement, while readymade art is composed of everyday objects. One example of Duchamp's kinetic art is called *Bicycle Wheel* (1913), in which a bicycle wheel is placed on top of a stool. He once used a bottle rack as an example of readymade art.

Although Duchamp's creative period was relatively short, his influence on the art world was great. Elements of Dadaism, Surrealism, and pop art can be traced directly to Duchamp. He was indeed a pioneer of modern art.

Duchamp eventually became an American citizen in 1955. On October 1, 1968, he died while in Paris.

Suggested Activities

Observe: Look at prints and photographs of Duchamp's work. Learn about the various artistic movements of which he was a pioneer, and determine how his pieces reflect those styles.

Paint: After learning about Duchamp's work, create a piece of art in Duchamp's style. After doing so, discuss whether or not modern art is as simple to create as many people suggest.

The Song-and-Dance Man

In 1878, in Providence, Rhode Island, George Michael Cohan was born. He would became one of the most famous men of World War I. More precisely, he became known for the era's most famous song, "Over There."

George M. Cohan

As a child, Cohan and his talented family performed in vaudeville as "The Four Cohans." When he was a teenager, he began to write vaudeville skits and songs himself. By the early 1900s, Cohan was one of the most popular people in the American theater. Throughout his long career, he wrote more than forty plays and musicals, producing, directing, and starring in most of them himself.

Cohan's work was particularly noteworthy for its high-spirited music and enthusiastic show quality. Generally, there was a patriotic flair and fervor to the music as well. It is no surprise then that his song entitled "Over There" became the most popular patriotic song—and perhaps the most popular song—during World War I. Everyone was singing it, and it was influential in encouraging many enlistees to sign up for military service overseas.

The plays of Cohan include *Broadway Jones*, *Seven Keys to Baldpate*, and *The Song-and-Dance Man*. However, his plays are not particularly remembered. It is the music of George M. Cohan that lives on in American culture. Songs such as "I'm a Yankee Doodle Dandy," "You're a Grand Old Flag," and "Give My Regards to Broadway" are classics of American popular music.

Cohan lived his life in the world of the theater. He died in 1942, a successful and prominent man.

Suggested Activities

Listen and Sing: Locate recordings of Cohan's music, being sure to include "Over There." (Cohan's music is easy to find, and there are many sources.) Play the music for the class. Learn the songs and sing them yourselves.

Vaudeville: Early in the century, vaudeville enjoyed great popularity. However, the movies finally put an end to vaudeville. Research vaudeville and some of its famous acts. If desired, have the class put on its own vaudeville show. Many old movies recreate vaudeville. Look to titles starring such celebrities as Judy Garland, Gene Kelly, Fred Astaire, and Donald O'Connor, and you will find many examples.

Stars: When vaudeville died out, many performers found new careers in the movies and on radio. Some later moved to television. Will Rogers, Burns and Allen, Bob Hope, Harry Houdini, Jack Benny, W. C. Fields, Milton Berle, and Edgar Bergen all began their careers in vaudeville. Choose one of these famous performers and trace his or her career after vaudeville.

Ragtime

Scott Joplin, the son of a former slave, loved music all his life. Born in Texarkana, Texas, in 1868, he left home at fourteen and traveled about the Mississippi Valley, playing piano in saloons. He wound up at the Maple Leaf Club in Sedalia, Missouri. In Sedalia, several of his compositions were published, including his famous "Maple Leaf Rag." During his lifetime, Scott Joplin wrote or collaborated on over sixty pieces of music and became a leading composer of what is known as *ragtime*, or simply rag.

Ragtime was very popular in the United States around the turn of the century and for the next several years. The term ragtime is short for "ragged time," and it refers to a type of music that is sometimes irregularly accented (or syncopated) and then regularly accented. The music is very energetic. Ragtime started as improvisational music, but composers like Joplin gave it a written form.

Scott Joplin

Ragtime was also the perfect music for some popular dances of the 1900s and 1910s, including the Turkey Trot, the Cakewalk, and the Grizzly Bear. These were dances designed to make children laugh, but they were also intended to be as different from traditional dance (such as the waltz) as possible. However, their strange and unprecedented movements had some people calling the dances indecent, immoral, and disgusting. These people said the same thing about ragtime music itself.

Though Joplin's life ended sadly and too soon (he died in 1917 in a mental hospital), he left a legacy of music that continues to delight and entertain. Joplin even received a special citation from the Advisory Board on the Pulitzer Prizes in the 1970s for his contribution to music. In fact, the seventies saw a revival of interest in his music due to a popular movie of the time called *The Sting*, which prominently featured Joplin's *The Entertaniner*.

Suggested Activities

Listen: In the classroom, listen to a recording of Scott Joplin's ragtime music. While listening, close your eyes and see what pictures come into your head as you listen. When the music is finished, quickly write down all the things the music made you think and feel. In small groups of three or four, share one of those things. Were your thoughts and feelings similar or very different?

Musical Match-Up: Music often accompanies scenes and events in movies, plays, and other productions. It is selected as a complement to a particular experience. What experience do you think ragtime would represent well? As a class, brainstorm some appropriate places and situations to play Joplin's music.

Dancing: A number of books on the history of dance will tell you about such popular dances as the ones listed above. Learn to do them as a class. Dance them while listening to some ragtime music.

Nijinsky

The 1910s saw the rise and fall of one of the most legendary ballet dancers ever known and the most popular male dancer of his time. His name was Vaslav Nijinsky.

Nijinsky was born in Kiev, Ukraine, in 1889. He began to study dance in 1898 at the St. Petersburg Imperial School of Ballet. He gained attention quickly, and he was asked to join Sergei Diaghilev's ballet company. In 1909, the company went to Paris to perform in Diaghilev's Ballet Russes. These were elaborate productions that featured stage designs

Vaslav Nijinsky

by such artistic masters as Matisse and Picasso and musical compositions by the world-renowned Ravel and Debussy. Nijinsky and the company were an enormous success. Crowds gathered for more of this amazing young star. The company traveled around the world, and everywhere they went, Nijinsky brought down the house. Although he was short with especially thick thigh muscles and a slope to his shoulders, his body seemed to lengthen and alter itself, depending on the roles he played. He became known for the incredible way in which he could master his body and his movements.

In 1913, Nijinsky married a fellow dancer, a ballet student with his company. This angered Diaghilev, and he dismissed his star male dancer. However, in 1916, Nijinsky once again joined with his old company, this time in the United States. His career flourished, and his dancing was up to the same quality it had been in years past.

Through the course of his career, Nijinsky created and choreographed a number of important roles, including those of Petrouchka and the faun in *The Afternoon of the Faun*. Many of his roles are still danced today, although it is a rare dancer who can attain Nijinsky's mastery. There is a famous story told of his skill. During the exit scene in *Le Spectre de la Rose*, Nijinsky is said to have risen slowly, leapt dramatically across a window ledge, and then stopped in midair—or so it seemed. The audience said that just as he stopped at the peak of his jump, he disappeared. Whether this story is true or not, it demonstrates the impact that Nijinsky's dancing and body control had on his audiences.

Sadly, by 1919, Nijinsky's career had come to an end. He suffered from mental illness, and by that year, he became completely insane. Though he continued to live for 31 years more, he would never perform again.

Suggested Activities

Video: View videotape of some modern ballet dancers, such as Barishnikov. Barishnikov's *Nutcracker* is wonderfully done and easy to find on video.

Ballet: Learn the five basic ballet positions. They can be found in any reference book on ballet.

Artists and Composers: Find out about Matisse, Picasso, Ravel, and Debussy. Look at and listen to some of their work.

Isadora Duncan

Isadora Duncan was the dance sensation of Europe from 1899 until her death in 1927. She almost single-handedly revolutionized classical dance, and she helped to bring about a new wave of modern dance.

Duncan was born in San Francisco in 1877. As a child, she loved to dance, but she refused to take ballet lessons. She found ballet too regimented and restrictive. She liked to dance naturally, in line with her own internal sense of rhythm and movement. Duncan believed that dance was an individual expression.

Her first dances were based on works of poetry that inspired her. She then became intrigued by literature, classical music, and figures from paintings and sculptures. She is perhaps best known for dancing that is based on forms from ancient Greek vases and mythology. Duncan also used nature as her inspiration, mimicking waves and other natural phenomena.

Isadora Duncan

Her style met with disapproval in the United States, so she moved to Europe at the age of 21 and performed there. Since she did not have much money, she sailed across the sea on a cattle boat. Once in Europe, she became a renowned innovator and dance sensation.

Isadora Duncan regularly danced barefoot in flowing, loose tunics. Her clothing was sometimes revealing, even see-through, and many people were shocked. On one occasion in Berlin, her performance was banned because the police said it was obscene. Duncan's private life was also shocking to many people, particularly Americans. She had many male companions, and her two children were born illegitimately. In 1913, a tragic and strange accident occurred. Her children were traveling in a car with their governess and a chauffeur. When the car broke down on a hill, the chauffeur got out. However, the car rolled back down the incline and into a river. The children, aged seven and five, and the governess were drowned.

Duncan's dancing brought her world fame, and in 1921, the new ruler of Russia, V. I. Lenin, invited her to live in Moscow. He even provided her with a house. While there, she taught dancing and established dancing schools for children in Russia, Germany, and France. She also married a Russian poet.

More tragedy came Duncan's way in 1925 when her husband hanged himself. Two years later, she herself died in a freak accident. While traveling in a car, her long scarf became wrapped in a spoked wheel of the vehicle. It immediately strangled her as the car sped forward.

Suggested Activities

Movement: Imitating Duncan's style, have the students move as things from nature might, such as waves, clouds, wind, and other phenomena.

Classical Art: Share pictures of some pieces of classical art with the students. Be sure to choose images that have figures on them. Ask students to mirror the images and to attempt to move as they might.

Jazz and New Orleans

Jazz is a style of music with its roots firmly planted in black history and culture. To understand the development of jazz, one must consider various traditions. Those traditions include the following:

- West African music and vocal styles, including improvisation, call-and-response patterns, complex and conflicting rhythms, and syncopated melodies
- Black folk music, including lullabies, blues, spirituals, and chants
- European music, including marches, waltzes, quadrilles, hymns, Italian opera, and harmony
- banjo music derived from minstrel shows (which, in turn, came from the banjo music of slaves)
- Latin-American music with syncopated patterns of rhythm
- barrelhouse piano music
- Black brass band music
- ragtime (a style combining syncopation with harmonies and contrasting patterns)

It is clear that jazz is not a simple or easily understood form of music.

Although various traditions can be found within the style known as jazz, it is difficult to trace its beginnings. What is known is that jazz began to appear in the music played by small marching bands and piano soloists. These musicians would play the familiar marches, hymns, and spirituals, adding and modifying the sound with syncopations and varied tempos. Elements of the blues and ragtime, two music styles which formed around the same time, became intermingled with the growing jazz movement. Both the blues and ragtime became components of the improvisation that is fundamental to jazz.

At the dawn of the new century, a style of jazz became documented in the New Orleans area. The trumpet, clarinet, and trombone were key to the melody and countermelody, with drums providing rhythm and the tuba or bass providing the bass line. With these instruments was combined something else: an energy and exuberance that became part of jazz's signature sound.

Although jazz developed prior to 1917, it was not until then that the first jazz recording was made. The record came from a New Orleans band of white musicians named The Original Dixieland Jazz Band. Their recording was enormously successful in the United States and abroad. Following this recording, two other bands came to the forefront of jazz music: the New Orleans Rhythm Kings and the Creole Jazz Band. The latter group was led by King Oliver, who played an important role in the development of jazz. King Oliver also gave the world one of the foremost pioneers of jazz: his second trumpeter, Louis Armstrong.

Considered to be the first virtuoso soloist in jazz, Armstrong understood the genre completely, improvising and developing the sound in ways that would set the standards for those to come. Among Armstrong's many accomplishments is the development of scat singing, a style of vocal intonations and sounds that mimic the improvised sounds of instruments.

In the twenties, many New Orleans musicians migrated to Chicago and then to New York, creating new jazz sounds and centers in each of those areas. Since then, jazz has continued to grow and develop, remaining just as strong and popular as in its early explosive roots.

Suggested Activity

Listen: Play various recordings from early jazz artists, particularly Armstrong. Also play some contemporary jazz musicians. Discuss the sounds.

America's Sweetheart

Mary Pickford

Born Gladys Marie Smith in 1893, Mary Pickford became the most popular actress of the early days of moviemaking. She was known as America's Sweetheart because of her huge popularity. In all, she appeared in 194 films.

Pickford's debut came in 1909. She grew to enormous popularity in the following years. Most notably, *The Poor Little Rich Girl* of 1917 made her one of the biggest stars of the time. *Rebecca of Sunnybrook Farm* of the same year was also a noteworthy film in her extensive career. Pickford's heroines were generally innocent and determined, fostering her image as America's Sweetheart—the ideal girl.

The actress won the Academy Award in the category of best actress for her performance in *Coquette*, a 1928 film. She also received an honorary Academy Award in 1976 for lifetime achievement.

In 1919, Pickford was one of the founders of United Artists, one of the first filmmaking companies in the new movie town, Hollywood. Her co-founders were actor Charlie Chaplin; director D. W. Griffith; and fellow actor and future husband, Douglas Fairbanks, Sr. At this time, she was earning a million dollars each year, an enormous sum. Pickford and Fairbanks were married in 1920.

When Pickford retired from moviemaking in 1933, she had made nearly 200 films in just 24 years. Mary Pickford, America's Sweetheart, died in 1979.

Suggested Activities

Silent Movies: Pickford's early days were in silent films. Have small groups each write and produce a short silent film. Play for them a silent film or two (some can be found on video), asking them to take note of the exaggerated expressions, title cards, and musical overlay. Their silent films can either be videotaped and played for the class or enacted in silent-film style.

In order to prepare their films, the students will need to do the following:

- Brainstorm for a story idea. Classic tales of good vs. evil are best.
- Outline the events of the story. Remember, they should be quite visual with little dialogue.
- Plan the text that will go on the cards.
- Prepare costumes and props.
- Rehearse.
- Dress in costume, ready the props, and roll film!

Viewing: If available in your area, rent a video copy of *The Poor Little Rich Girl* or *Rebecca of Sunnybrook Farm*. Both are acceptable for students.

Music: Music has always played an important part in moviemaking, adding to the emotional content of the story. Give the students a list of emotions (happy, sad, angry, fearful, etc.) and ask them to find instrumental music that conveys each of those emotions. You may wish to do this as a class exercise, collecting samples of music the students bring in and determining as a class what they signify. It would be interesting to have the students write down an emotion while they listen to the music. Make a class chart showing what each person has written and compare responses.

Fanny Brice

Fanny Borach was born on October 29, 1891, in New York's lower east side. Her parents, Charles Borach and Rose Stern, were a saloonkeeper and a real estate agent, respectively.

Fannie always had a love for song and dance. As a child she performed in her father's bar, and at the age of thirteen, after winning a contest, she sang to her own piano accompaniment in a movie theater. Always demonstrating a strong comic bent, Brice began to do burlesque and used parody in the songs she performed.

In 1910, Max Spiegel asked Fanny, now using the name Fanny Brice, to perform in *The College Girls* in a large New York theater. He also asked her to perform in a benefit he was producing. In order to do her best, Brice asked Irving Berlin to write songs for her performance. One of the songs, "Sadie Salome, Go Home," became a signature song throughout Brice's career. The song tells of a Jewish girl whose family is shocked by her life on stage. While performing the song, Brice used a Yiddish accent. A Yiddish dialect became a regular part of Brice's routine.

Many prominent people in the world of theater saw her performance in Spiegel's shows. One of them, Florenz Ziegfeld, was so enamored of her that he offered her a role on Broadway in his popular *Follies* of 1910. In the following year, Brice joined the vaudeville circuit and went on tour. When her tour closed, she performed at the Victoria in New York and the Victoria Palace in London. Many writers and directors were drawn to this talented and funny impresario, and her career blossomed with a number of roles on Broadway such as Jerome Kern's *Nobody's Home*.

The year 1916 saw the return of Brice to the *Ziegfeld Follies* where she performed the funny and popular piece "The Blushing Bride." She continued with the *Follies* until 1924. When her run with Ziegfeld was complete, she had performed in four revues and seven editions of the *Follies*.

Although an attractive, graceful, and talented woman, Brice would exaggerate her imperfections and carry herself in such a way as to make the audience laugh while at the same time endearing herself to them. She would also often parody popular performers of the day, such as the Barrymores. Her comic talents became renowned. However, Brice did have a straight side as well. One of her most remembered songs is "My Man." During the performance of this song, Brice would lean against a lamppost, singing about her devotion to a man who had brought her untold pain. While singing this song onstage, offstage Brice was going through a similar pain. Her husband, Nickie Arnstein, was imprisoned for embezzlement.

In 1924, Brice left Ziegfeld and returned to vaudeville, also taking roles in a number of films, including *My Man* and *Sweet and Low*. It was in the latter film that she introduced the character called Babykins, a precursor to Baby Snooks, another role that would become signature Brice.

Health concerns began to plague Brice, so she left the stage for Hollywood. In 1936, she created a radio show starring Baby Snooks. The show ran for ten years. In 1946, she appeared in MGM's *Ziegfeld Follies*, the only actual star of the *Follies* to do so.

In 1964, a new Broadway show hit the stage, starring Barbra Streisand. It was called *Funny Girl*, and it told the story of Fanny Brice. The movie version followed in 1968. Through the play and movie, Fanny Brice has become immortalized.

Brice died on May 19, 1951, due to a cerebral hemorrhage. She was 59 years of age.

Suggested Activity

Movies and Radio: Locate recordings of Brice's radio show or rent a copy of *Ziegfeld Follies*. Write reviews of Brice and the *Follies*.

The Father of the Motion Picture

David Wark Griffith was born in 1875 in La Grange, Kentucky, and he received a standard education for the time and place. Always exhibiting an interest in theater, he worked as an actor in stock theater and road companies. In 1908, he became a film actor for the Biograph Film Company. Later, he became a director for the same company. Amazing by today's standards, D. W. Griffith made 450 films for Biograph. It is for this and for the full career that followed that Griffith became known as the Father of the Motion Picture.

It was with Biograph that Griffith began to gather a pool of talented professionals, including such actors and actresses as Wallace Reid, Mary Pickford, the Gish sisters, Mabel Normand, and Mae Marsh, and such directors as Mack Sennett and Erich von Stroheim. Also among his connections was the pioneering cameraman, Billy Blitzer. Griffith left Biograph in 1913. He went to Reliance-Majestic Studios for awhile, and then he began to produce films independently. In 1914, he created the successful film *Judith of Bethulia*. He followed this movie with one that remains as controversial today as it is significant. It was *Birth of a Nation*. Made in 1915, it told a Civil War story, demonstrating sympathy for the Confederate perspective. While the subject matter is controversial, the film is considered by many to be the original modern film and among the most important of all time. It was the first feature-length film, and it also was the first to use a star system, which has become part of the Hollywood infrastructure. Nonetheless, the film's racist perspective incited protests and riots upon release. For this reason, the film was also instrumental in helping to create film censorship laws.

By the time Griffith made *Intolerance* in 1916, his reputation as a leading producer and director of films was cemented. This particular film also had a strong influence in creating the concept of film art. Prior to Griffith, films were generally produced in a very different manner. They were short and episodic with two-dimensional characters rather than fully developed and dramatic stories with rich and vivid characterizations. With Griffith's film, the quality of the production and the performances were also enhanced. Griffith also pioneered several film techniques, including the following: **close-up**—close view of a face or body for dramatic purposes; **fade-out**—gradual fade of one scene while transitioning to the next; **cutback** (also called flashback)—shows scenes that came before the events of the film in order to clarify current action; **parallel editing**—crosscutting footage from various angles or simultaneous action in order to heighten viewer suspense.

Griffith also changed the face of moviemaking when, in 1920, he joined Mary Pickford, Charlie Chaplin, and Douglas Fairbanks to create United Artists Corporation, a company created to produce movies. Rather than being directed by studio management that did not take part in the creative process, United Artists was a production company created by and for the creative team. Griffith directed many films for United Artists, including *Broken Blossoms* (1919), *America* (1924), and *Lady of the Pavements* (1929). All of these films were silent (except for the latter one which contained some singing). Griffith did make two talking films, *Abraham Lincoln* (1930) and *The Struggle* (1931), but they never achieved the success of his silent films.

After a long, successful, and influential career, D. W. Griffith died in 1948.

Suggested Activity

Movies: Watch one of the films created by D. W. Griffith and others from the era. Some of these movies are available on videotape.

End of the Wild West

In 1917, an era came to an end with the death of Buffalo Bill, a legend of the Old West. Today, Buffalo Bill's exploits are controversial, but at the time he was a celebrity of great stature.

Born William Frederick Cody in 1846, Buffalo Bill spent his lifetime in a number of occupations throughout the Western frontier, and in the decades prior to his death, he was a national showman. Here is the story of his life.

Buffalo Bill Cody

When Cody was eight years old, his family moved from his birthplace of Le Claire, Iowa, to Kansas. His father died when he was eleven years old, and Cody began to work. First, he was a messenger for a freight firm. He took a year off to attend school, and then he traveled with wagon trains going west, first as a caretaker of livestock and then as a horse driver. In 1860, he was a rider for the legendary, but short-lived, pony express.

The Civil War followed, and Cody joined the Union Kansas Militias and the Ninth Kansas Volunteers. He was also a teamster in the Seventh Kansas Volunteer Cavalry. When the war ended in 1865, Cody became a hotel operator and a freighter; however, he lost his wagon and horses to Indians. He tried land speculation and railroad construction as well, but he became famous as a hunter of buffalo. After killing the animals, he would provide their meat to the railroad in order to feed the men building the rails across Kansas. Cody proved to be an excellent and prolific shot with his rifle, and so the workmen on the railroad lines nicknamed him "Buffalo Bill." In fact, it is said that he killed over 4,000 buffalo in just 18 months.

In 1868, Cody became a scout for the military while they battled with the Indians in the West. He also served as a guide for buffalo hunters. In 1872, he took part in a battle between Indians and the military on the Platte River, for which Congress awarded him the Medal of Honor (which they later rescinded because Cody was not then a member of the military).

It was in 1872 that Cody began his career on the stage. Theaters across the nation hosted the "Wild West" show starring Buffalo Bill Cody. It was a big success. Cody followed it in 1883 with "Buffalo Bill's Wild West," which ran for 30 years. It included demonstrations by Cody and by other Western figures, such as the sure-fire shot Annie Oakley. Oakley was noteworthy at the time for having shot the ash from a cigarette in the mouth of Germany's Kaiser. Buffalo Bill's show traveled throughout the United States and in parts of Europe. He performed until shortly before he died.

In 1894, Cody moved to a home in the Bighorn Basin of Wyoming. He died in 1917 and was buried on Lookout Mountain near Denver, Colorado. His passing served as a reminder that the Old West had truly died.

Suggested Activities

Out with the Old: The Western frontier was no longer wild by the turn of the century, but fragments of the Old West remained for a number of years. Find out about some of the other final figures from the Old West.

Buffalo: Cody took part in the mass killings of buffalo; this behavior nearly made buffaloes extinct. Research to find out about this practice and its effect on the native people of the land.

Show Time: Prepare a show depicting a certain time and place, such as Buffalo Bill's show did about the Wild West. Have the students prepare different skits under a central theme. Preferably, choose a time from the twentieth century. In this way, the students will learn about history as they prepare their skits.

Father's Day

When Sonora Louise Smart Dodd of Spokane, Washington, heard a sermon at her church concerning Mother's Day, she got the idea for a day to honor fathers in the same way. Dodd wished especially to honor her own father, William Jackson Smart, who had raised his six children alone after his wife died in 1898.

The young woman began a petition recommending that Spokane adopt an annual Father's Day celebration. She also got the support of the Spokane Ministerial Association and the Young Men's Christian Association (YMCA). Dodd's efforts were finally successful, and on June 19, 1910, the first Father's Day was celebrated in Spokane.

After that time, many people and groups tried to make the day a national holiday; it was not until 1972, though, that President Richard Nixon signed the day into law.

Today, Father's Day is celebrated around the world. In the United States and Canada, it falls on the third Sunday in June. On that day, people honor their fathers with gifts, cards, and special tributes.

Suggested Activities

Fathers: Have the students write poems, make cards, or create other pieces of art to honor their fathers. Also discuss what it is that makes a good father. Let the students share their views.

Holidays: Research to determine the origination of several national holidays. Have the students brainstorm for additional holidays they feel would be worthwhile. Have them focus particularly on the people they think should be honored.

My Dad Is: In the space below, let the students free-write the continuation of the words "My Dad is. . . ." Instruct them to write without stopping to think; have them record whatever comes to mind. These free-writes may make nice Father's Day gifts.

My Dad is . . . _____

_____

_____

_____

_____

_____

_____

_____

_____

What's New?

Like every decade, the 1910s were filled with new and popular ideas, inventions, and styles. Here are some of them.

Raggedy Ann: The popular doll was created by political cartoonist John Gruelle at the request of his terminally ill daughter. Eight-year-old Marcella Gruelle found an old rag doll in the family attic in 1915. The doll was faceless, so she took it to her father. He drew a face on the doll and asked his wife to restuff it. She did, and she added the now-trademark heart to its chest. The heart read, "I love you." The redheaded rag doll quickly became famous nationally, and soon every little girl wanted her own Raggedy Ann.

Life Savers: In 1912, a candy maker from Cleveland developed a peppermint candy with a hole in the middle. He called it a Life Saver since it resembled a life preserver.

Oreos: A new cookie was developed in 1912. It was made of two chocolate wafers sandwiching a cream filling. It was named the Oreo Biscuit, and it was developed by the National Biscuit Company (now Nabisco).

Cranberry Sauce: Today's Thanksgiving dinner would not be complete were it not for the Ocean Spray Cranberry Company in 1912. In that year, they first produced cranberry sauce, a sweetened jelly made from cranberries.

Jazz: In 1917, it was spelled *jass*, but it was still the exciting music known today by its free-flowing, syncopated sound. It was said to have been developed in New Orleans by black musicians who had extended it from ragtime, blues, and other musical forms. The Original Dixieland Jass Band was the first to use the word officially.

Lincoln Logs: John Wright, the son of famous architect and designer Frank Lloyd Wright, developed Lincoln Logs in 1916 so that children could build their own structures. He got the idea while watching the construction of a hotel in Tokyo.

Hobble Skirts: Women in 1910 were seen to hobble around due to their new fashion. Hobble skirts were made very tight at the ankle so that women could not move freely. The style caused such an uproar that the pope condemned it publicly.

Tango: Also in 1910, a new dance craze shocked the clergy. It was called the tango, and it was a romantic dance that alternated short, quick steps with long, low ones.

Kinetophone: Thomas Edison's latest invention of 1910 combined sound and picture recording. "Talking pictures" were just around the corner.

Suggested Activities

Research: Choose any one of the items listed above and research to find more details about its development. Also attempt to find early advertising of the products or depictions of the dances or styles.

Brainstorm: As a class, brainstorm for the new items that you think will still be popular in the next century.

68

The Look of the Times

The look of the times was full and colorful but a tad less flamboyant than the last decade and certainly more practical. Women's hemlines were raised to just above the ankles, while girls' dresses were knee length. Waists were slightly dropped, and blouses were gathered in the front to create the "pouter pigeon" look. Shoes were pointed and often high-topped. Bobbed hair became all the rage as young women began to break from tradition, joining the work forces in large numbers to become "working girls." During the war years, red, white, and blue became the prominent colors of American fashion, and women were encouraged to makeover old clothes to help support the war effort.

Here and on the next page are some typical outfits from the era. Use them to study or to color.

Challenge: Design other clothing in typical 1910s styles.

The Look of the Times *(cont.)*

Men customarily wore suits with spats and high-topped shoes. Suit styles varied little from the previous decade, although many men naturally began to wear military uniforms. In fact, uniforms would begin to influence the style of civilian clothing. Men usually wore hats, although the hats were not as fanciful as women's. Boys' clothes were similar to men's, although boys often wore short pants.

Elsewhere

This chronology gives a few of the important events around the globe during the 1910s. Have students research further any people and events that interest them.

1910
- The Mexican Revolution begins.
- South Africa becomes a dominion of Great Britain.
- George V comes to the British throne.

1911
- The Russian premier is assassinated.
- There is revolution in China.
- Roald Amundsen reaches the South Pole.

1912
- The German-Italian-Austrian Alliance is renewed.
- Montenegro declares war on Turkey.
- Bulgaria and Serbia engage their military forces.

1913
- The Balkan War erupts.
- King George I of Greece is assassinated.
- Suffragettes in London demonstrate.

1914
- Archduke Ferdinand of Austria is assassinated.
- Germany declares war on Russia, France, and Belgium. World War I begins.
- The Panama Canal is opened.

1915
- Germans first use the submarine.
- The *Lusitania* is sunk.
- Zeppelins are used to bomb London.

1916
- Tanks are used for the first time on the Western Front.
- Gas masks and steel helmets are used for the first time by the Germans.
- Britain introduces the use of Daylight Saving Time.
- The Olympic Games are cancelled due to the war.

1917
- Tsar Nicholas II of Russia abdicates.
- Germans begin to withdraw on the Western Front.
- Mata Hari is executed as a German spy.

1918
- The Armistice between Germany and the Allies is signed on November 11, ending World War I.
- The Russian tsar and his family are executed.
- Women in Britain get the vote.

1919
- The Peace Conference begins in Versailles, France.
- Benito Mussolini founds the Fascist Party.
- The Bauhaus is founded in Germany.

Passages

Births

1910
- Sy Oliver, American jazz composer

1911
- Phil Silvers, American comedian
- Lucille Ball, American actress

1912
- Charles Addams, American cartoonist

1913
- Richard Nixon, United States president
- Albert Camus, French author
- John Mitchell, U.S. attorney general
- Danny Kaye, American actor

1914
- Tennessee Williams, American dramatist
- Pierre Balmain, Parisian fashion designer

1915
- Saul Bellow, American novelist
- Arthur Miller, American dramatist
- Orson Welles, American filmmaker

1916
- Keenan Wynn, American actor
- Jackie Gleason, American actor and comedian

1917
- John Fitzgerald Kennedy, United States president
- Ferdinand Marcos, Philippine president
- Buddy Rich, American jazz drummer

1918
- Billy Graham, American evangelist
- Leonard Bernstein, American composer and conductor
- Rita Hayworth, American actress

1919
- Sir Edmund Percival Hillary, New Zealand explorer
- An Wang, American founder of Wang laboratories
- Malcolm Forbes, American publisher and businessman

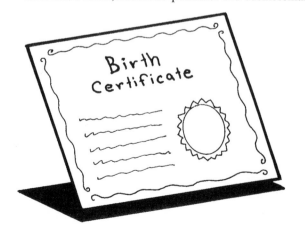

Deaths

1910
- King Edward VII, king of England
- Mark Twain, American author and humorist
- Count Leo Tolstoy, Russian novelist and philosopher
- Mary Baker Eddy, founder of Christian Science
- Julia Ward Howe, American writer and suffragist
- Henri Rousseau, French painter
- Florence Nightingale, noted American Civil War nurse

1911
- W. S. Gilbert, librettist

1912
- August Strindberg, Swedish dramatist

1913
- Harriet Tubman, American abolitionist and freedom fighter
- King George I, Greek monarch
- J. P. Morgan, American financier

1914
- Archduke Francis Ferdinand, heir to Austrian throne
- Pope Pius X, Roman Catholic leader

1915
- Rupert Brooke, English poet
- Booker T. Washington, American educator
- W. G. Grace, English cricketeer

1916
- Henry James, American novelist
- Rasputin, Russian monk
- Thomas Eakins, American artist

1917
- Edgar Degas, French artist
- Auguste Rodin, French sculptor
- Count Ferdinand von Zeppelin of Germany
- "Buffalo Bill" Cody, American hunter and showman

1918
- Claude Debussy, French composer

1919
- Theodore Roosevelt, United States president
- Sir Wilfred Laurier, first French-Canadian prime minister of Canada
- Louis Botha, South African general and statesman
- W. W. Campbell, Canadian poet
- A. D. Juilliard, founder of Juilliard School of Music in New York
- Andrew Carnegie, American industrialist and philanthropist
- Frank W. Woolworth, founder of the American five-and-ten-cent stores

End of an Empire

At the onset of World War I, the Ottoman Empire was a sprawling entity, spreading throughout the continents of Africa and Europe. It was ruled by an elite group of Turks, although the Turks were a minority. By the end of the war, the more than 600-year reign of the Ottoman Empire would end.

In 1908, a small group of Ottoman military officers, called the Young Turks, became frustrated with the Ottoman Empire. Once, briefly, a democracy had existed there with a democratic constitution. The new ruler, Abdul-Hamid II, had accepted the constitution when he came to power in 1876; but by the next year, he had suspended it and ruled with complete authority. The sultan modernized the Ottoman Army in order to fortify his authority; however, the new army would eventually lead to his own destruction. Abdul-Hamid's rule came to an end in 1909 when the rebels forced his abdication and deposed him. The new Turkish army remained strong, and to this day, it plays an important part in the politics of the nation.

About this time, segments of the Empire were being taken over by other nations. Britain had gained control of Egypt and Cyprus, adding them to its growing British Empire. The British also encouraged dissension among the Arab tribes in the Arabian peninsula, part of the Ottoman Empire. France took the tiny nation of Morocco, and Libya went to Italy.

The new leaders of the Empire chose to become allies with the rising powers of Germany. This helped them for a time, but eventually it proved to be the downfall of their world. The battles of World War I became more than the new leadership could handle, and British soldiers and guerrillas bested them in the end.

The last European segments of the Ottoman Empire were the Balkan states. In 1912 and 1913, there was an internal power struggle in the Balkans. This struggle would eventually spark the greatest war the world had ever known. When Archduke Franz Ferdinand of Austria-Hungary was assassinated, the fallout between Serbia and Bosnia caused nations around the world to take sides and to battle for the Balkans as well as each other's territory.

During the course of the rebellion and war, a holocaust occurred in Armenia to rival the later holocaust of Jews in Europe. Tragically, millions of Armenians were murdered by leaders struggling for power in the shaky Empire. The Armenians were wiped out in a battle for control and autonomy with prejudice and hatred at its base. This massacre foreshadowed the infamous one that was already brewing in Germany and its surrounding nations.

The Turks lost the war in 1918 to British troops under the leadership of British General Edmund Allenby and the legendary British officer known as Lawrence of Arabia (page 74). When Germany was finally defeated and the peace terms were agreed upon, the Ottoman Empire was completely disbanded. Only death and destruction remained in its place.

Suggested Activities

Cartography: Draw maps of the Ottoman Empire, coloring in and labeling the significant nations.

Holocaust: Learn more about the Armenian massacres of the early 1900s. Also, find out about the status of Armenia today.

Lawrence of Arabia

Victory came to the British in Turkey in 1918 under the leadership of General Edmund Allenby and an archeologist named T. E. Lawrence. Although Allenby was the true hero of the war in Turkey, it was Lawrence who gained legendary status. He became known as Lawrence of Arabia.

Thomas Edward Lawrence was born in Tremadoc, Wales. In his early adulthood, he studied archeology, the Near East, and the Arabic language at Oxford University in England. He then took employment with the British government as an archeologist.

When World War I began, T. E. Lawrence was sent to head the military intelligence department in Egypt. He was eventually made a colonel in the British Army. As such, he worked with the Arabs to lead a revolt against the Ancient Ottoman Empire (page 73). It was during this time that he developed a deep affinity with the Arab cause and took it as his own. Lawrence became an expert at guerrilla warfare, and he was instrumental in the Arabs arrival in Damascus, the capital of Syria, which became the final turning point in the war for the Turks. Allenby also arrived in Damascus at the same time.

Thomas Edward Lawrence

After the war, Lawrence refused all honors the military and the Arabs wished to bestow upon him. However, he was hailed as a hero by the British and Arabs alike. The Arabs called him "the uncrowned king of Arabia."

When the peace treaty negotiations began in Versailles, Lawrence went to plead the cause of the Arabs. They wished to be an independent nation. However, he failed to convince the other negotiators.

After the war, Lawrence was made an adviser to Arab affairs by the British Colonial Office, but he resigned a year later, displeased with the fame and notoriety he had achieved. In 1922, he joined the Royal Air Force (R.A.F.) under the pseudonym J. H. Ross, but his true identity was discovered. He then joined the tank corps under the assumed name T. E. Shaw, and in 1925, he returned to the R.A.F. as Shaw, legally changing his name.

It is strange that after surviving so many years of adventures and dangerous guerrilla exploits, the legendary Lawrence of Arabia finally died in a motorcycle accident in England. The year was 1935.

Suggested Activities

Movie: View the film *Lawrence of Arabia*, a classic of American cinema. Determine if and how the movie differs from the true story of T. E. Lawrence. As with any film, view it first before sharing it with your class and be sure to get approval from your administration and students' parents.

Cartography: Draw maps of the principal nations involved in Lawrence's World War I adventures. They include Judea, Palestine, Syria, and Turkey.

Read: Lawrence published a book in 1926 called *The Seven Pillars of Wisdom*. A shortened version called *Revolt in the Desert* was published in 1927. In them, the author tells of his exploits in Arabia. Try to locate copies or excerpts from the books and share them with the class.

Roald Amundsen and the South Pole

Roald Amundsen was born in Borge, Norway, in 1872. He received a college education at the University of Christiania (now the University of Oslo) and then joined the Norwegian navy. For the next nine years, Amundsen studied science intensely.

Amundsen always had a love of exploration and discovery. From 1903 to 1906, he was finally able to lead his first expedition. During this voyage through the Northwest Passage between the Atlantic and Pacific Oceans, he was able to determine the position of the North Magnetic Pole.

Amundsen's second expedition was from 1910 to 1912. Together with his assistants, Amundsen lived in Antarctica for more than one year, conducting experiments and studying the geography and terrain of the area. To this day, Amundsen's Antarctic expedition is heralded as one of the greatest Antarctic endeavors of all time, for it is on that journey that Amundsen and his team became the first known individuals to reach the South Pole. The date was December 14, 1911.

Amundsen's success is credited to a number of factors. He was lucky enough to enjoy favorable weather conditions, but there was a great deal more to it than that. Amundsen was renowned for his attention to detail as well as his extensive knowledge of the polar area and conditions. Additionally, Amundsen was in excellent physical condition and had a natural ability to endure physical stress.

Amundsen next planned an expedition to the North Pole; however, the outbreak of World War I interrupted his plans. After the war, in 1918, Amundsen attempted to drift across the North Pole with the ice currents of the Arctic Ocean. However, the theory did not work in practice, and Amundsen had to change to a route through the Northwest Passage. This expedition ended in 1920 when Amundsen reached Nome, Alaska.

Amundsen tried once more in 1922 to reach the Pole by ship and by airplane; however, he was again unsuccessful. In 1924, Amundsen tried to raise funds for another expedition, and this time his endeavors paid off. In May 1926, with the aid of American explorer Lincoln Ellsworth and Italian explorer Umberto Nobile, Amundsen crossed the North Pole on a flight that took more than seventy hours from Norway to Alaska. The plane was designed and constructed by Nobile, who was also an engineer, working with the support of the Italian government. After their successful flight, Nobile and Amundsen disagreed over whose country should get credit for the flight. The two parted in anger. However, in 1928, Nobile's plane was wrecked, and Amundsen came out of retirement to find his former partner. Although Nobile was rescued, Amundsen and his crew disappeared on June 28, 1928. The wreckage of their plane was found on August 31.

In addition to exploration, Amundsen also wrote and lectured. His books include *North West Passage* (1908), *The South Pole* (1912). *The North East Passage* (1918–1920), *Our Polar Flight* (1925, with Lincoln Ellsworth), *First Crossing of the Polar Sea* (1927, with Lincoln Ellsworth), and *My Life as an Explorer* (1927).

Suggested Activities

Geography: Learn about the Antarctic Circle and the South Pole. What must travel have been like for Amundsen in the 1910s?

Robert F. Scott: Amundsen beat Scott and his party to the South Pole by five weeks. Learn more about Scott and this great race to the Pole.

Robert E. Peary: Amundsen had had hopes to reach the North Pole first, but Peary beat him to it. Learn more about Peary and his expedition to the North Pole.

Trotsky

Leon Trotsky might have been the leader of the Union of Soviet Socialist Republics, but it was not to be. Instead, he was second in command to Lenin, and he later lost power to Joseph Stalin. Nonetheless, he was an important and influential leader in the politics of Russia and the new U.S.S.R.

Born Lev Davidovich Bronstein in the Ukraine in 1879, Trotsky was the son of wealthy parents. By his teens, he had become part of a revolutionary movement in Russia and spent two years as a Social Democrat. In 1898, he was arrested and sent to Siberian exile. He escaped to London in 1902, and it was there that he met V. I. Lenin. Trotsky followed Lenin's lead and changed his name so as to be undetected by the Russian government.

Leon Trotsky

In 1905, Trotsky returned to Russia and took part in the revolution there. Due to his leadership of the St. Petersburg Soviet in 1905, he was once again arrested. He escaped in 1907 and spent the next ten years in Western Europe as a revolutionary writer and editor. When World War I began, France and Spain expelled Trotsky, and he went to New York.

In 1917, while in New York, Trotsky heard of the fall of the tsar (pages 17 and 18). He returned to Russia and, once again, joined Lenin. Together, they plotted and achieved the Bolshevik takeover in October (November by today's calendar) of 1917. Trotsky was appointed by Lenin as the first Soviet commissar of foreign affairs. Next, he became the first Soviet commissar of war.

Civil war followed in Russia in 1918–1920, and Trotsky organized the powerful Red Army. He became a prominent leader in the newly formed U.S.S.R., second only to Lenin. When Lenin died, most people believed that Trotsky would step into his place. However, another leader, Joseph Stalin, outwitted Trotsky and usurped his place.

In 1927, Trotsky was expelled from the Communist Party. In 1928, he was exiled to Soviet Central Asia, and he was deported to Turkey in 1929. From there, he moved to Norway and finally to Mexico. In 1930, while in Mexico, he published his life story, entitled *My Life: An Attempt at an Autobiography*.

In 1940, Stalin decided that he had been too lenient on Trotsky, who had continued to battle the U.S.S.R. leader from overseas. Stalin sent an agent of his secret police to Mexico to assassinate the former leader. On August 21, 1940, Trotsky was murdered.

Suggested Activities

Read: A book entitled *Leon Trotsky* by Hedda Garza (Chelsea House, 1986) is suitable for students. In it, they can learn more about the life of this influential leader. Older students will enjoy George Orwell's *Animal Farm*, an allegory of the Russian Revolution with animals representing the various Bolshevik leaders, including Trotsky, Stalin, and Lenin.

Autobiography: Trotsky made "an attempt at an autobiography." Have the students do the same, writing their own life stories and publishing them in self-made books.

German Leaders

Kaiser Wilhelm II and Paul von Hindenburg were two prominent German leaders who came to international recognition and infamy throughout the course of World War I.

Kaiser Wilhelm II: The last emperor of Germany, Kaiser Wilhelm II was also the nephew of Britain's monarch, King Edward VII, and the cousin of Tsar Nicholas II of Russia. King Edward and the Kaiser did not get along, and both took part in an arms race during the 1900s and into the 1910s. This arms race eventually contributed to the outbreak of World War I. The Kaiser received most of the blame for the war, although today it is believed that the Russians and Austrians were equal partners in its inception.

Although he was paralyzed in his left arm, the Kaiser hid his infirmity and ruled with tremendous authority. Under his leadership, Germany grew in prosperity and boosted its trade and manufacturing. His empire also grew with the addition of colonies in Africa and on islands in the Pacific Ocean. The Kaiser built an army and navy that were virtually unrivaled. It was these achievements that brought Germany into conflict with the British Empire.

Under the Kaiser's reign, Germany broke an alliance with Russia, which eventually forced the nation to fight World War I on two fronts, against both the British and the Russians as well as their allies.

The Kaiser was noted around the world for his brutality and ruthlessness in war. Even people in his own nation were known to oppose his hardline tactics. In 1918, the German navy mutinied, and internal revolution broke out. On November 7 of that year, the prime minister of Germany demanded the abdication of the Kaiser, and two days later, Wilhelm II gave up his throne. He fled to the Netherlands, a neutral country in world politics, where he lived in comfortable exile until his death in 1941.

Paul von Hindenburg: Von Hindenburg was Germany's military leader during World War I, and from 1925 until his death in 1934, he was the nation's president. It was Hindenburg who appointed Adolf Hitler as chancellor in 1933.

Hindenburg was a military hero who became a general in 1896 and retired in 1911. When World War I began, he came out of retirement to command the German Eighth Army. General Erich von Ludendorff became his second in command, and the two went on to win many victories for the powerful German Army. In 1916, Hindenburg was named supreme commander of all German forces.

In 1917, Hindenburg created the Siegfried Line to shorten the Western Front and to ease the burden of Germany's soldiers. The line—called the Hindenburg Line by the Allies—held fast for more than a year. The Allies eventually broke it in September 1918, and that brought about the end of the war.

As president, Hindenburg lost ground to the growing Nazi party, but he used his power to keep Hitler out of control. However, by 1932, the Nazis had the strongest control, and Hindenburg was forced to give Hitler the position of chancellor on January 30, 1933. When Hindenburg died in 1934, Hitler dismantled the presidency and became the supreme authority.

Suggested Activity

History: Trace the line of Germany's political leadership throughout the twentieth century.

"You Are the Man I Want"

Horatio Herbert Kitchener, first Earl of Khartoum and of Broome, was born in County Kerry, Ireland, in 1850. He was educated at the Royal Military Academy at Woolwich. His military skills were sharpened over the years in Palestine, Cyprus, Egypt, and South Africa. It was during World War I, however, that he gained international fame. As the British secretary of war, Kitchener's face was immortalized on thousands of recruiting posters with such captions as "You Are the Man I Want," "Your Country Needs You," and "[picture of Kitchener's face] Wants You: Join Your Country's Army." Kitchener's recruitment program developed an extensive British army, highly significant to the eventual victory by the Allies. In all, three million men enlisted for duty at the Western Front.

Horatio Herbert Kitchener

Kitchener is considered to be the last great military hero of Britain. Highly trained as an army engineer, Kitchener demonstrated exceptional talent for detail, planning and organizing attacks, and defense. However, he was at heart a soldier, and he thrilled in the battle.

In 1871, France and Germany were at odds, and Britain was neutral. A young army officer at the time, Kitchener secretly went off to take part in the conflict, almost creating an international incident. Another time, while on sick leave, he went to Egypt, where growing tensions were leading toward war. Notoriety came to him at the end of the nineteenth century for his actions as second in command during the Boer War of South Africa. His efforts played a major part in victory there. He then became commander of the South African army and brought victory despite long battles against guerilla warfare.

Kitchener served as governor general of the Sudan and commander of the Egyptian Army. His leadership toppled the Dervishes, an aggressive religious group fighting for power at the time. Kitchener also reoccupied Khartoum for the British army, an area they had previously gained but lost. He served as commander in chief to the British army in India, and he was influential in Australia and New Zealand in bringing about reforms to their armies. After serving as head of the British administration in Egypt, Kitchener was made Earl of Khartoum and Broome in 1914. It was at that point that he was made secretary of war for the British.

A brave and strong leader for the first two years of the war, Kitchener made a voyage to Russia in 1916 to meet with the tsar about new battle tactics. However, his ship struck a mine in unswept waters, and Kitchener was drowned. His death was an untimely shock to the struggling British who looked to him for leadership and victory. He was replaced as secretary of war by David Lloyd George.

Suggested Activities

History: Learn more about the history of the British army.

Recruiting: Design modern-day recruitment posters. What figures and images do you think would prove successful in encouraging young people to enlist for active war duty?

Spies and Aces

Several figures came to prominence during the Great War, not for their leadership but for their legendary qualities. Three such figures were Mata Hari, the Red Baron, and Eddie Rickenbacker.

Mata Hari: Margaretha Geertruida Zelle was born in Leeuwarden, Netherlands, in 1876. She grew to become the popular exotic dancer Mata Hari. Mata Hari began dancing in France after her marriage failed. Her style was exotic, and she pretended to be Javanese. Quickly, her fame spread throughout Europe, and she became noted for her strange and sensual dances.

Mata Hari's dancing began to lose popularity after a while. At that time, she apparently became involved with a network of German spies with whom she is said to have worked during World War I. The French discovered her treachery, and in 1917, they executed her on charges of spying for the Germans.

The Red Baron: On April 21, 1918, the World War I flying ace known as the Red Baron finally met his end. Baron Manfred von Richthofen was considered by his native Germany to be a modern-day knight of the sky. During World War I, he gunned down 80 enemy planes. The world came to know him as the Red Knight or, more popularly, the Red Baron, because of his red airplane.

The Red Baron was noted for his exceptional flying skill and the bravery with which he maneuvered. Upon his death, Allied soldiers gathered souvenirs from his plane. Although he fought for the enemy, the Allies also formed an honor guard at the Red Baron's funeral.

Eddie Rickenbacker: Captain Eddie Rickenbacker was the top American flying ace during World War I. In 1918, he was recognized for having shot down 22 planes and four observation balloons in just six month's time. Fourteen of his victories (downed planes) came in just one month. Rickenbacker did not begin to fly until he was 26 years old, one year before he joined the United States Army Air Service.

As a child, Rickenbacker was poor. He had to drop out of school when his father died. It was very unusual for a fighter pilot in World War I to be poor and uneducated. However, Rickenbacker had ambition. He became an expert auto mechanic and race car driver. In fact, he suggested to the United States military that they employ race car drivers as their fighter pilots. The military ignored him, saying they thought it was ridiculous for him to think he could learn to fly at such a relatively late age. But he did, and the rest is history.

Suggested Activities

Spies and Aces: Every modern war has known a number of spies and flying aces. As a class, find out about some of the most famous and what they did. Put their stories together in a book of war heroes and villains.

Java: Mata Hari pretended to be a dancer from Java. Locate the nation on a map. Find out about its government, culture, and customs.

Barons: A baron is a level of aristocracy in some European nations. Find out what this classification means as well as other titles of distinction, such as earl, duke, viscount, and so forth.

Aces: The term "ace" originated in World War I. Research to determine what it means and how a person qualifies as an ace. (There *are* official guidelines.)

Fascism

The Fascist Party that saw its glory days in the mid-twentieth century had its beginnings in the 1900s and 1910s with a man who came to be known as Il Duce (the leader), Benito Mussolini.

Mussolini was born in Dovia, Italy, in 1883. For a short time, he was an elementary school teacher. In 1902, he developed an interest in socialism. He then served in the Italian military from 1905 to 1906, and afterwards he became a socialist leader, working for a socialist newspaper in Austria. However, the Austrians expelled him from their country because of his revolutionary tendencies.

In 1912, Mussolini became the editor of the official socialist newspaper in Italy. He used the paper to encourage Italian involvement in World War I; however, many in the Socialist Party disagreed with him. Mussolini decided to resign from that paper and to found his own. In 1914, he began *Il Popolo d'Italia*, again using the paper to encourage Italian participation in a war against Germany and Austria. Mussolini was expelled once more, this time from the Socialist Party.

Benito Mussolini

Italy did enter the war in 1915. Mussolini served in the Italian Army from 1915 until 1917, when he was wounded. He spent the next two years building upon his ideas and developing a new way of thinking. Out of this came Fasci di Combattimento (Combat Groups), the foundation of Mussolini's new party. It would come to be known as the National Fascist Party in 1921. Mussolini's movement encouraged Italian interests and patriotism as well as government ownership of all resources. It also supported warlike policies and the persecution of minorities. In the 1920s, the Fascists used violence to combat opposing parties.

Mussolini's goal was to make Italy a major power in the world, rivaling the greatest empires. Fortunately for the world, his plans did not prove successful. After World War II, the people of his own country executed him.

Suggested Activities

Cartography: Draw maps of Italy before World War I and in the modern day. How do they differ?

Fascism: Research to find out more about the Fascist party and its rise and fall in Europe. Compare it to Naziism.

History: Find out about the Italian government since the era of Mussolini.

Dictators: Research to learn about other dictators in history. You can also hold a class experiment. Investigate what government is like under dictatorial leadership. Appoint a student or group of students to be the class dictators. Establish a period of time for their rule. Then switch and have the dictators be the governed and vice versa. Afterwards, have the class discuss their experiences.

Bauhaus

The brainchild of an architect named Walter Gropius in 1919, the Bauhaus of Germany was a world-renowned school of design that had an enormous influence on modern architecture, design, graphic art, and industrial art. Constructed in Weimer, Germany, the Bauhaus was created as the merging of a traditional art academy and the more functional techniques and philosophy of the new arts and crafts school. This philosophy was originated by William Morris, a 19th century designer who believed that art should be useful, meeting the needs of society. Morris (and later Gropius) felt that there should be no distinction between fine arts and practical arts. Furthermore, as the world became more industrialized, Gropius thought that art should respond, becoming both aesthetically pleasing as well as structurally sound.

Because of Gropius' philosophy, the Bauhaus offered classes in arts and crafts, commercial design, industrial design, typography, and the traditional studies of painting, sculpture, and architecture. At the time, no other school made such an offering.

From the school there came a style, the Bauhaus style, which was characterized by an absence of ornamentation and a balance between artistry and engineering. Gropius designed a set of glass and concrete buildings in this style in the area of Dessau. In 1925, the school was moved to its new site. There the Bauhaus style became even more dramatically bare and functional. Beauty was said to come from the simplicity of the materials.

The Bauhaus in its prime was able to boast a lofty staff. Among those working at the school were the painters Paul Klee, Wassily Kandinsky, Laszlo Moholy-Nagy (who would later found the Chicago Institute of Design on this same philosophy), Lyonel Feininger, and Oskar Schlemmer.

The school moved to Berlin in 1932 under the directions of Ludwig van der Rohe. However, by the following year the school had been closed by the Nazi Party. Fortunately, the Bauhaus and its philosophy by that time were world renowned.

As turmoil erupted in Germany and war broke out, many members of the Bauhaus staff immigrated to America. The teachings they brought with them served as a springboard to the architectural style known as International.

International style was the most prominent architectural trend in the thirties and forties. It came directly from the Bauhaus as well as from the Constructivists of Russia, the Dutch movement of De Stijl, and the changing demands of urban development. International style, like Bauhaus style, is geometric and functional. Concrete, steel, and glass are common building materials within this style because they are not only practical and useful but also appealing in their simplicity.

The Bauhaus and International styles can be seen most evidently in the countless skyscrapers that began to appear in their times as well as in the large factories and apartment buildings that needed to be functional for matters of productivity and limited space. The Bauhaus style can still be seen in the buildings left behind as well as in the dramatic influence the style has had on modern architecture.

Suggested Activities

Architecture: Study the history of modern architecture. Focus on some renowned architects such as Frank Lloyd Wright. How were these architects and styles influenced by the Bauhaus?

Design a School: Imagine you could design a school for any educational purpose, just as Gropius did in creating the Bauhaus. What would your school teach? What would it look like? Describe your school in writing and then draw it.

Mexican Revolution

The 1910s were filled with revolution in Mexico. The nation saw several leaders during that time and a great deal of bloodshed.

Porfirio Díaz was the Mexican dictator in 1910, but opposition to him had been growing for the past decade. In the 1910 election, Francisco I. Madero chose to run in opposition to the dictator. Díaz had his opponent jailed until after the election. Díaz won, and Madero fled to the United States.

Madero had always opposed violence, but he saw no other way to rid the nation of the dictator than through revolution. In November of 1910, Madero called for revolution in Mexico. Several bands of revolutionaries sprang up throughout the nation. In May of 1911, Díaz's own government officials forced him from office in order to halt further revolutionary bloodshed. Madero, the Father of the Mexican Revolution, became president that year.

However, Mexico was split into many factions by this time, and Madero could not bring them together. In February of 1913, Madero was murdered by the forces of General Victoriano Huerta, who then seized power. Mexico was once again split in its loyalties. Many people, hoping for an end to the violence, supported Huerta. Others put their support behind Venustiano Carranza, a state governor. The United States also stood in support of Carranza, openly opposing the murder of Madero and halting economic aid to Mexico.

At this time, seamen on an American ship docked in a Mexican port were arrested for no reason. Although they were released and an apology was issued, the United States demanded a twenty-one-gun salute to the American flag. Huerta refused. American marines and sailors swarmed on Vera Cruz and captured the city. Nineteen Americans were killed and 126 Mexicans lost their lives. In July 1914, the United States and Carranza succeeded in overthrowing Huerta, who was forced to leave the country.

Carranza's government soon split in its own battle for power. Out of the revolution came two rebel leaders, Francisco "Pancho" Villa and Emiliano Zapata. They each led rebel forces in Mexico, vying for control and fighting Carranza's rule. In 1915, the United States stopped the export of guns to Carranza's opposers. In revenge, Pancho Villa raided the small American town of Columbus, New Mexico, killing eighteen Americans and burning the town. President Woodrow Wilson sent General John J. Pershing across the border to capture Villa. The army trailed Villa for 300 miles, angering the Mexican government by their interference. However, Villa eluded capture.

In 1916, Carranza's government was recognized by most of Mexico, and in 1917, a new constitution was adopted. However, Carranza did not follow through on the laws of the constitution, and revolution broke out once more. In 1920, Carranza was killed by General Alvaro Obregon's rebellion. Obregon later became president of Mexico.

The United States abruptly withdrew from involvement in Mexico in 1917, just when it seemed full-scale war between the two nations could not be avoided. America's full attention was on Europe where it was about to enter World War I.

Suggested Activities

Cartography: Draw a map of Mexico and the United States.

History: Trace the intertwined history of Mexico and the United States, focusing on where the two nations stand in relationship to one another today.

Pancho Villa

Born Doroteo Arango in Rio Grande, Francisco Villa—commonly called Pancho Villa—is one of the most famous and influential leaders of revolution in Mexico. When revolution erupted in Mexico in 1910 against the dictator Porifirio Diaz, Villa immediately aligned himself with the rebel leader, Francisco I. Madero.

The history of the revolution is basically this: Madero was a well-educated landowner who strongly urged the populace to overthrow Diaz's regime. In 1908, his publication entitled *La succession presidencial en 1910* (*The Presidential Succession in 1910*) strongly urged voters not to support Diaz. Diaz's government attempted to suppress the book; however, it was circulated extensively. Madero became Diaz's primary opponent; however, Madero was arrested and imprisoned for allegedly inciting a revolt, and Diaz won the election. Upon his release in late 1910, Madero fled to Texas. While there, he called for a revolution. In 1911, the revolutionaries captured Ciudad Juarez, forcing the resignation of Diaz. Madero became provisional president and, in May of that year, was elected outright. However, revolution broke out again in 1912, and General Victoriano Huerta overthrew Madero in 1913. Madero was imprisoned and killed, allegedly while trying to escape.

While Madero was in office, Pancho Villa served under General Huerta. However, Villa broke ranks with Huerta and was sentenced to death for insubordination. The outlaw escaped to the United States, but he came back to Mexico after the assassination of Madero. The new opposition to the government was led by Venustiano Carranza, and Villa quickly joined his forces. As in the past, however, Villa and his leader grew in opposition to one another. When Carranza came to power in 1914, it was Villa who led the rebellion against him.

At this time, the United States chose to recognize Carranza as the legal president of Mexico. In outrage over this recognition, Pancho Villa came to New Mexico and killed a number of its citizens, destroying part of the city in the process. The United States quickly took action against him, but a detail led by General Pershing was not able to find him. Fearing that the United States might turn against him, Carranza ordered the U.S. military out of his country.

When Carranza was likewise overthrown, Pancho Villa finally decided to accept the new government. He went into retirement in Parral, Chihuahua. It was while there in 1923 that the longtime revolutionary was assassinated.

Suggested Activities

Geography: Learn about the geography of Mexico.

History: Learn about the geographic histories of the United States and Mexico in relationship to one another.

Revolution: Compare the revolution in Mexico with other revolutions such as America's Revolutionary War in 1776.

Panama Canal

For many years, sailors had wished for a shortened way to navigate their ships from the Pacific Ocean to the Atlantic. At the turn of the century, the journey took 7,000 miles (11,270 kilometers). However, beginning on August 15, 1914, it became a trip of 40 miles (64.4 kilometers).

Panama is a small nation lying at the base of Central America and at the northwest corner of Colombia, South America. Its area is relatively narrow. In the 1880s, the French attempted to build a canal across the nation, but their plans were ineffective. They also had to deal with rampant jungle diseases such as malaria and yellow fever. France gave up its efforts.

In 1904, the United States, under the leadership of President Theodore Roosevelt, gained the rights to build a canal through Panama. The project began with a vengeance. Americans arrived in Central America by the thousands, hoping to capitalize on high wages. However, the problems of disease and climate were the same for the Americans as they had been for the French. In order to succeed, different tactics had to be taken.

President Roosevelt hired a chief engineer, General George W. Goethals, to head the project. Goethals and his team developed a system of locks that would raise and lower the water level for the passage of ships. General William Gorgas, an Army physician, was brought on board to curb the effects of malaria and yellow fever. Although he was not able to stop the diseases, he did reduce the death toll from 39 per thousand workers in 1906 to 7 per thousand workers by 1914. However, throughout the project, nearly six thousand workers died.

The entire project required the removal of 240 million cubic yards of earth. The number of workers employed reached, at its peak, 40,000, and the cost for the project, which took ten years to complete, was more than $350 million.

Finally complete in the summer of 1914, the Panama Canal let pass its first ship, the *Alcon*, on August 15 with a shipload of officials on board. As they sailed the meager miles from ocean to ocean, no one seemed to mind the toll the canal had taken, and they rejoiced during the 15 or so hours it took to sail completely through the passage. Although the canal could never repay the lives lost, it has more than repaid the financial costs. Today, approximately 70 ships pass through the canal each day at a cost of approximately $7,000 in tolls.

Suggested Activities

Cartography: Draw Panama and the location of the canal on a map. Also draw a map showing the route that needed to be taken by ships prior to the canal's completion in 1914.

Disease: Find out about malaria and yellow fever and how they were treated in the years of the Panama Canal's construction. Also find out how they are treated today.

Research and Discussion: Find out the importance to the United States of the Panama Canal. Determine why it was considered worth spending lives and money in order to construct the Canal. Discuss what you find.

History: Trace the history of the Canal from the time it was built until the present. Does the United States still maintain rights to the Canal?

1910–1919 Facts and Figures

Make a copy of the chart below for each pair of students. Direct them to use the information on this page as a comparison with a chart (page 86) they will complete about the current decade.

The United States in the 'Teens

Popular Books: *Howard's End, A Boy's Will, Ethan Frome, The Innocence of Father Brown, Riders of the Purple Sage, Doctor Doolittle, O Pioneers!, Tarzan of the Apes, Ulysses, Of Human Bondage, Chicago Poems,* war memoirs (various authors)

Popular Entertainers: Charlie Chaplin, the Barrymores (Lionel, John, and Ethel), Sarah Bernhardt, Fanny Brice, George M. Cohan, Isadora Duncan, Mary Pickford, Enrico Caruso, Mata Hari

Popular Movies: *Carmen, Cleopatra, Birth of a Nation,* all Charlie Chaplin films

Popular Songs: "Over There," "Till We Meet Again," "Maple Leaf Rag," "Memphis Blues," "Alexander's Ragtime Band"

Fashions: *(women)* pouter pigeon look, high-topped shoes, pointed toes, Louis XIV heels, leggings, feathered hats, dropped waists, hems just above the ankle, bobbed hair, practical clothes for working; *(men)* spats, leggings, high-topped shoes, simple hats, sack suits, ties, vests, suspenders, military uniform influences

Fads: neon signs, lunatic fringe (bangs), Erector Sets, tennis, zippers, the cakewalk (a dance), military style in clothing, Raggedy Ann dolls, hobble skirts, the tango

New Products, Technology, and Programs: airmail stamps, jazz music, zippers, Oreo cookies, Life Savers®, cranberry sauce, Hollywood movies, talking movies (kinetophone), mechanical air conditioner, electric self-starter for autos, city airport, transcontinental telephone service, tanks, submarines, poison gas, Boy Scouts of America and Campfire Girls, Father's Day, assembly lines, the Panama Canal

Popular Artists: Paul Cézanne, Auguste Rodin, Marcel Duchamp, Pablo Picasso, Frank Lloyd Wright (architect), Henri Matisse, Vincent van Gogh

Popular Writers: G. K. Chesterton, Edith Wharton, Hugh Lofting, Willa Cather, Upton Sinclair, Jack London, Zane Grey, James Joyce

Sports Stars: Jack Dempsey, Jim Thorpe, Ty Cobb, Jack Johnson, Denton T. "Cy" Young, Knute Rockne, May Sutton, Mrs. Hillyard

Popular and Influential Figures: Thomas Edison, Roald Amundsen, George Washington Carver, Albert Einstein, Robert Falcon Scott, Robert Peary, Charlie Chaplin, Theodore Roosevelt, Henry Ford, T. E. Lawrence

Comparing the Times

With a partner, fill in the blanks on this page. Compare your answers with the information on page 85.

Popular Books: _____

_____

Popular Entertainers: _____

_____

Popular Movies: _____

_____

Popular Songs: _____

_____

Fashions: *(women)* _____

        (men) _____

Fads: _____

_____

New Products, Technology, and Programs: _____

_____

Popular Artists: _____

_____

Popular Writers: _____

_____

Sports Stars: _____

_____

Popular and Influential Figures: _____

_____

Famous Firsts

In the 1910s, the United States saw the first

. . . celebration of Father's Day.

. . . electric self-starting for cars from General Motors.

. . . Indianapolis 500 automobile race.

. . . identification of vitamins.

. . . aircraft takeoff from the deck of a ship.

. . . senators elected by popular vote.

. . . income tax.

. . . wireless telegraph message sent across the Atlantic Ocean.

. . . legalized celebration of Mother's Day.

. . . establishment of the U.S. Coast Guard.

. . . skyscrapers built in New York.

. . . National Park Service.

. . . transcontinental telephone call.

. . . Tournament of Roses football game.

. . . Pulitzer Prize.

. . . airmail stamps and airmail service.

. . . municipal airport.

. . . jazz music.

. . . Oreo cookies, Life Savers, and cranberry sauce.

. . . neon signs.

. . . Hollywood movie studios.

. . . black world heavyweight boxing champion.

. . . woman elected to the U.S. House of Representatives.

. . . ship sail through the Panama Canal.

. . . talking movies (with Edison's kinetophone).

. . . president to throw out the first ball in the baseball season.

. . . female licensed pilot.

. . . birth control clinic.

. . . constitutional right to vote for women.

. . . constitutional prohibition of the sale of alcohol.

. . . mechanical air conditioner, designed by W. H. Carrier.

What Year Was That?

Check how well you remember the second decade of the twentieth century by circling the correct year for each event.

1. Woodrow Wilson proposed his Fourteen Points.
   1917   1918   1919

2. Revolution breaks out in Mexico.
   1910   1911   1912

3. The NAACP is founded.
   1910   1911   1912

4. The *Titanic* sinks.
   1910   1912   1916

5. World War I breaks out.
   1914   1915   1916

6. The United States declares war.
   1916   1917   1918

7. The Armory Show creates a stir in New York.
   1911   1912   1913

8. Amundsen reaches the South Pole.
   1910   1911   1912

9. Tsar Nicholas and his family are killed.
   1916   1917   1918

10. *Birth of a Nation* causes protests and riots when it premieres.
    1915   1916   1917

11. T. E. Lawrence leads Arabs into Damascus.
    1917   1918   1919

12. The Triangle Shirtwaist factory burns.
    1910   1911   1912

13. Henry Ford first uses the assembly line.
    1913   1914   1915

14. The first transcontinental phone call is made.
    1914   1915   1916

15. Jack Johnson defeats Jim Jeffries.
    1910   1911   1912

16. The Grand Canyon National Park is established.
    1917   1918   1919

17. World War I ends.
    1917   1918   1919

18. Woodrow Wilson wins his first presidential election.
    1910   1911   1912

19. Vitamins are identified.
    1912   1913   1914

20. The "Black Sox" scandal shocks the nation.
    1917   1918   1919

Into the Twenties

The tumultuous decade of 1910–1919 was rocked by war, and as the world moved into the twenties, there was hope for peace, order, and renewal. In fact, when Warren Harding campaigned for the presidency in 1920, he promised a "return to normalcy." For most Americans, this meant a return to life as it had been before the war; but the war had changed the nation and the world too much to go back to the way things were.

Harding's brief administration is remembered for its corruption, especially the Teapot Dome Scandal. After Harding's untimely death in 1923, Calvin Coolidge was sworn into office. Believing that "the chief business of America is business," Coolidge shepherded tax laws through Congress that were mostly favorable to businesses. In 1928, Herbert Hoover, who promised "four years of prosperity," won the presidency by a landslide. After the stock market crash of 1929, Hoover was largely blamed for the disaster.

Prohibition became the law of the land in 1920. No one is certain whether drinking increased during Prohibition or not, but it did spread among women and youth and became a symbol of defiance. It also gave rise to organized crime and increased violence. Bootlegging was a big business.

While American law had always been in support of an "open door" immigration policy, by 1921 overcrowding had become so significant that quota laws were instituted. Many Americans feared they might lose their jobs to newcomers who were willing to work for less pay. Others were suspicious of foreigners with different customs and languages.

By the end of the twenties, many families had automobiles—a novelty at the beginning of the decade. Radios brought nightly comedy shows and news to families throughout the country and changed political campaigns. People flocked to the movies, which, starting in 1927, even had sound.

Musicians George Gershwin and Aaron Copeland, writers Earnest Hemingway and F. Scott Fitzgerald, and artists Mary Cassatt and Grant Wood became prominent. In the predominately black-populated section of Harlem in New York City, the Harlem Renaissance produced a host of great African-American writers, artists, and musicians.

Fostered by presidents who favored business, the stock market reached new heights before the crash on October 29, 1929. At first, President Hoover believed that the situation was temporary and refused to allow government aid for homeless and out-of-work people. His seeming insensitivity to the plight of the American people cost him the election of 1930.

Literature Connections

Literature Ideas: The following books can be used to supplement and enhance the study of the 1910s.

- ***All Quiet on the Western Front*** by Erique Maria Remarque (Little, Brown and Company, 1929)

  Originally published in German, this novel tells of a group of young German soldiers fighting the last days of World War I. The novel is especially realistic and poignant because the author was, in fact, a drafted soldier for the German Army. As the author writes in the preface of the book, "I will try simply to tell of a generation of men who, even though they may have escaped its shells, were destroyed by the war." Remarque left Nazi Germany in 1932 and settled in the United States.

- ***Rilla of Ingleside*** by Lucy Maud Montgomery (J. B. Lippincott Company, 1921)

  Eighth in the series of books beginning with *Anne of Green Gables*, *Rilla of Ingleside* tells the story of Anne's youngest daughter, Rilla Blythe. Rilla is fifteen years old when World War I breaks out in Canada's mother country of England. Her brothers and friends enlist to fight as British citizens. The story tells of the war experience from the perspective of the people back on the home front. A great deal of detail about the people and events of the war is included, but it is all interwoven with the feelings and efforts of the families and friends waiting for the war to be over and for their young men to return home. The story includes its share of tragedy, but as in all the Anne novels, there is always a strong human spirit that rises above adversity.

- ***War Game*** by Michael Foreman (Arcade, 1994)

  Set in France in 1914, this book tells the story of four English friends who enlist in the army. The boys are sent to the Western Front and posted as sentries very close to the German trenches. Barbed wire, dead bodies, and devastation surround them; but on Christmas Eve an impromptu truce is observed. The armies take turns serenading one another with Christmas carols. On Christmas Day the peace is continued as the men shake hands, bury the dead, and then engage in a soccer game. Days later, however, the fighting resumes. This book is somewhat based on actual events.

Extensions

Read and Review: Read any of the books on this page and prepare a review to present the book to the class. Be sure to state a clear opinion about the book and support your ideas.

Let's Go to the Movies: After reading one of these books, create a movie poster advertising the "film version." Be sure to show a significant image that will demonstrate the theme of the movie. Also include the title. Add other touches as you choose.

My Story: After reading one of these novels, write a short story of your own that tells about a World War I experience. Write the story in the first person. Add details to show your understanding of the time and place.

Act It Out: After reading one of the novels, be prepared to be interviewed by the class as the main character of the book. One at a time, class members can take turns being the lead characters. Others in the class can ask questions about the character's life and experiences. The questions can refer to actual things stated in the book or they may require some creative thought in order to be answered.

Writing Prompts

Use these suggestions for journal writing or as daily writing exercises. Some research or discussion may be appropriate before assigning a particular topic.

- You are a soldier on the Western Front during World War I. Write a page from your diary.

- You are in your home town in 1917, waiting for your older brother to return from war. Write a page from your diary.

- As a child laborer in a large New York factory in 1912, you suffer low wages, long hours, and poor working conditions. Write a conversation you have with the children working near you.

- You are in the room while the Treaty of Versailles is being negotiated. Describe what happens.

- Pancho Villa is the leader of your gang of rebels. One evening, you are all sitting around a campfire in the Mexican desert. Write the conversation you share.

- Write a speech from the perspective of a suffragette demanding the vote.

- Write a speech that President Wilson might have given Congress to convince them to join the League of Nations.

- You are part of the crew on the *Titanic*, and you survive the wreck. Tell your account to a newspaper reporter.

- You are ringside as Jack Johnson defeats Jim Jeffries. Describe the scene as well as the crowd.

- You receive the first transcontinental phone call from Alexander Graham Bell. Write your conversation.

- You want to bob your hair and your mother will not allow you to do it. Write your conversation as you try to persuade her.

- You are a reporter covering the Black Sox scandal. Write your story.

- You are touring the famous Bauhaus school of art in Germany. Describe what you see.

- Roosevelt has decided to run against Taft, the same man he hand-picked to replace him. Write a conversation that Roosevelt and Taft might have had.

- You witness Jim Thorpe's amazing success at the 1912 Olympics. Describe what you see.

- You are there when Thorpe's medals are taken back. Write an argument for or against this action.

- Imagine that a kindergarten is opening in your school for the first time. What do you think should be taught there?

- Write a letter to the president from a citizen of New Mexico or Arizona, urging statehood.

- You attend the very first Indianapolis 500 race. Describe what you see.

Me in 1910

Imagine yourself at your present age in 1910. Complete the following prompts, using what you imagine to fill in the blanks.

Where I live: _____

_____

What my home is like: _____

_____

What I do when I get up in the morning: _____

_____

_____

What a typical school day is like: _____

_____

What I do for fun: _____

_____

_____

My chores: _____

_____

How my family spends our evenings: _____

_____

_____

Buzzwords

New inventions, habits, lifestyles, and occupations cause people to invent new words. The second decade of the new century was no exception. Listed below are some of the words and phrases that came into popular use throughout the decade.

Ace: This term, which originated in France during World War I, denotes aviators who shoot down at least five enemy aircraft during war. The downing must be confirmed by an eyewitness or be recorded on film in order to qualify.

Airplane: Originally *aeroplane*, this is an aircraft kept aloft by aerodynamic force.

Allergy: This refers to a condition of unusual sensitivity to a substance, often characterized by systemic disturbances.

Backpack: This word for a type of knapsack, usually attached to a frame and worn on the back of a hiker, originated during World War I.

Big shot: This is a slang expression denoting someone who is influential.

Camouflage: First used during World War I, this word came from the French *camoufler*; it means to disguise or to change the appearance of people or things to protect them from being sighted by the enemy.

Cellophane: This is a thin, transparent product made from cellulose.

Collage: This is a type of art in which bits of flat materials are pasted together onto a surface.

Cutting remark: This slang expression suggests a comment made to emotionally injure an individual.

Dog tag: This is a term for a military identification tag worn by a soldier around the neck. It comes from the tag's resemblance to an identification tag on a dog's collar.

Intelligence test: This refers to a standardized series of questions or problems meant to test an individual's intellect.

It's a cinch: This slang expression means that something is done with ease.

Jazz: This type of music originated with New Orleans black musicians and was often improvisational.

Joyride: This is slang for a trip by motor car taken just for the joy of riding.

Lousy: This slang term means bad, foul, or inferior.

Lowbrow: This term of contempt designates an individual lacking a high degree of cultural knowledge or intellectual prowess.

Lunatic fringe: This term originally was slang for hair bangs; now it means an extremist or irrational member of a group.

Movie: A shortened form of moving picture, this word refers to films.

Peachy: This is slang for fine or excellent.

Pinch hit: This term comes from baseball and means to bat in the place of the regular player when a hit is especially needed.

Radio station: This is a building with equipment for broadcasting radio waves.

Spill the beans: This slang expression means to tell a secret, especially accidentally.

String along: This slang expression means to hold someone's interest without satisfying his desire.

Sure: When used as slang, this word means certainly.

Software in the Classroom

More and more software is finding its way into the classroom. Many of the multimedia packages allow students to access photos, speeches, film clips, maps, and newspapers from various eras in history. Although a program may not be written specifically for the topic you are studying, existing software may be adapted for your purposes. To get maximum use from these programs and to learn how to keep up with technology, try some of the suggestions below.

Software

American Heritage: The History of the United States for Young People. Byron Press Multimedia.
American History CD. Multi-Educator.
Chronicle of the 20th Century. Dorling Kindersley Ltd.
Compton's Encyclopedia of American History. McGraw Hill.
Compton's Interactive Encyclopedia. Compton's New Media, Inc.
The Cruncher. Microsoft Works.
Encarta (various editions). Microsoft Home.
Ideas That Changed the World. Ice Publishing.
Our Times: Multimedia Encyclopedia of the 20th Century (Vicarious Points of View Series 2.0). Scholastic.
Presidents: A Picture History of Our Nation. National Geographic.
Time Almanac. Compact Publishing (available through Broderbund, 800-922-9204).
TimeLiner. Tom Snyder Productions (800-342-0236).
Time Traveler CD! Orange Cherry.
Vital Links. Educational Resources (includes videodisc and audio cassette).
Where in America's Past Is Carmen Sandiego? Broderbund.

Using the Programs

After the initial excitement of using a new computer program wears off, you can still motivate students by letting them use the programs in different ways.

1. Print out a copy of a time line for the first decade for each group of students. Assign each group a different topic—for example, entertainment or politics. Direct the groups to research their topics and add text and pictures to their time line.

2. Let each pair of students choose a specific photo from the first decade of the twentieth century. Have them research the person or event and write a news story to go with it.

3. If you do not have enough computers in your classroom, hook your computer to a television screen for whole-class activities and let the students take turns typing. Keep a kitchen timer handy. For more ideas, see *Managing Technology in the Classroom* (Teacher Created Materials).

Internet

If you have access to the Internet, let the students search for related information. First ask the students to brainstorm a list of keywords or topics. Use a Web browser such as Alta Vista or Web Crawler to search for sites. Facts, pictures, and sound clips are only a click away. As an alternative, you may wish to preview sites and provide students with a list of URLs for access.

Note: If the students will be searching, you may wish to install a filtering program, like SurfWatch from Spyglass, to limit access to objectionable material. Check with your Internet service provider.

Bibliography

Aaseng, Nathan. *You Are the President.* Oliver Press, Inc., 1994.

Adler, Susan S. *Meet Samantha: An American Girl.* Pleasant Company, 1986.

Davis, Kenneth C. *Don't Know Much About History.* Crown Publishers, 1990.

Denam, Cherry. *The History Puzzle: An Interactive Visual Timeline.* Turner Publishing, 1995.

Duden, Jane. *Timelines.* Crestwood House, 1989.

English, June. *Transportation: Automobiles to Zeppelins.* Scholastic, 1995.

Felder, Deborah G. *The Kids' World Almanac of History.* Pharos Books, 1991.

Grun, Bernard. *The Timetables of History.* Simon and Schuster, 1991.

Hakim, Joy. *All the People.* Oxford University Press, 1995.

Hopkinson, Christina. *The Usborne History of the Twentieth Century.* Usborne Publishing, 1993.

Kranz, Rachel. *The Biographical Dictionary of Black Americans.* Facts on File, 1992.

Lane, Rose Wilder. *Old Home Town.* University of Nebraska Press, 1985.

London, Jack. *The Call of the Wild.* Watermill, 1980.

MacBride, Roger Lea. *The Rose Years: On the Banks of the Bayou.* HarperCollins, 1998.

Montgomery, L. M. *Rilla of Ingleside.* Scholastic, 1989.

The Oxford Children's Book of Famous People. Oxford University Press, 1994.

Platt, Richard. *The Smithsonian Visual Timeline of Inventions.* Dorling Kindersley, 1994.

Rubel, David. *The Scholastic Encyclopedia of the Presidents and Their Times.* Scholastic, 1994.

—*The United States in the 20th Century.* Scholastic, 1995.

Sharman, Margaret. *Take Ten Years: 1910s.* Steck-Vaughn, 1994.

Skarmeas, Nancy. *First Ladies of the White House.* Ideals Publications, 1995.

Smith, Carter. *Presidents in a Time of Change.* The Millbrook Press, 1993.

Tames, Richard. *Picture History of the 20th Century: 1900-1919.* Franklin Watts, 1991.

—*What Happened Next?: Great Events.* Franklin Watts, 1995.

Tierney, Tim. *American Family of 1900-1920: Paper Dolls in Full Color.* Dover, 1991.

Teacher Created Materials

#064 *Share the Olympic Dream*

#069 *Elections*

#234 *Thematic Unit: Immigration*

#517 *Managing Technology in the Classroom*

#605 *Interdisciplinary Unit: Heroes*

Answer Key

page 29

1. 48
2. 17,667,827
3. 1,545
4. 515
5. 531
6. 15,415,820
7. 30%
8. 17%

page 48

1. machine gun
2. 120-mm gun
3. ammunition
4. frontal armor
5. continuous track
6. engine and transmission
7. driver
8. gunner
9. commander
10. loader

page 88

1. 1918
2. 1910
3. 1910
4. 1912
5. 1914
6. 1917
7. 1913
8. 1911
9. 1918
10. 1915
11. 1918
12. 1911
13. 1913
14. 1915
15. 1910
16. 1919
17. 1918
18. 1912
19. 1912
20. 1919